Why Study Mysteries?

What are the answers to the mysteries in ancient history? Who invented the alphabet? Were King Tut and two others murdered in ancient Egypt? Was there really a horse in Troy? Why was Stonehenge built, and who were its builders? Did Atlantis exist long ago as a prosperous nation? Why did the great emperor of China create terracotta soldiers, and how did he do it so secretly? Did a real King Arthur ever exist? What are the mysterious lines in South America? Who erected the statues on Easter Island, and for what reason were they erected? How did the iceman die? Will we ever really know the truth to these mysteries? Probably not—and that is precisely what makes these mysteries so useful to us today.

Why should we ask questions that cannot be answered with absolute certainty? Asking these types of questions demands that students speculate, debate, gather evidence, judge, evaluate, and compare. In this process, students use higher-level thinking skills. Their capacity to think critically increases with each new ambiguity. This book is designed to help students think critically. At first, these lessons might frustrate the student who always wants the one right answer. But as teachers learn to handle these frustrations and encourage students to think for themselves, students will grow to love these types of stories where there is not one right answer. In addition, these lessons enable students the opportunity to generate creative products like news-magazine articles, write a story, analyze theories with a game, write a play, participate in a court case, create a travel brochure for visitors, design a cereal box with a historical figure, analyze lines with popular polls, and create a documentary.

How This Book Is Organized

There are ten mysteries in this book. While the activities vary within each mystery, the layout for implementing the lessons is the same. Each mystery begins with an attention grabber. Some of these are in the form of a primary-source-like diary entries and newspaper articles, and others are eye-catching posters and simulations. Students have the opportunity to discuss these attention grabbers. Each mystery also has a graphic organizer so that students can keep track of what they are learning. Every piece of background information needed for each mystery is provided in this unit. Teachers will not need to research beyond what is provided here. If students want to look into other aspects of the mysteries, resources are available in the bibliography at the end of the unit. The activities vary within each mystery. One has students put on a trial, another allows students to work for a newspaper, and yet another lets students work as investigators. Each mystery allows students to become the experts. They pull together pieces of information and make the final decision on the mystery, while providing evidence as support for their view.

Who Invented the Alphabet?

Teacher Lesson Plans

Standard/Objective

✻ Apply knowledge of how groups and institutions work to meet individual needs and promote the common good. (NCSS)

✻ Students will analyze information about early alphabets, create a semantic map about its possible origins, and write a story about how the alphabet came to be that records what they believe is the truth.

Materials

copies of *Attention Grabber* (page 7); copies of *Graphic Organizer* (page 8); copies of *Background Information* (pages 9–11); copies of *A Map of the Region* (page 12); copies of *A Timeline of the Alphabet* (page 13); copies of *Comparison of Ancient Languages* (pages 14–15); copies of *The True Story of the Alphabet* (page 16)

Discussion Questions

✻ What is the meaning of this story?

✻ Why would someone write a story like this one?

✻ Do you think this story is a true account? Why or why not?

✻ For what reasons would an author write a story like this if it were not true?

✻ If this story were true, in your opinion, how would that change history?

The Activity: Day 1

Begin class by telling students that they will have a story time this morning. Divide students into small groups (3 or 4 per group) and give them copies of *Attention Grabber* (page 7). Explain that they will be reading in small groups. After they read, they will be answering some questions about the meaning of the story. Let students decide how they will read this short synopsis of Rudyard Kipling's *How the Alphabet Was Made*. Some groups may take turns reading, while others may decide to designate a reader for their group. Give students a few minutes to finish reading and then post the discussion questions on the board or on an overhead projector. Tell students to talk about these questions in their groups. When all groups have had a chance to read and discuss, allow each group to give their best answers to the class and hold a classroom discussion about the story.

Editor
Eric Migliaccio

Managing Editor
Ina Massler Levin, M.A.

Illustrator
Sue Fullam

Cover Artist
Brenda DiAntonis

Art Manager
Kevin Barnes

Art Director
CJae Froshay

Imaging
Rosa C. See

Publisher
Mary D. Smith, M.S. Ed.

MYSTERIES in HISTORY

Ancient History

Grades 5-8

Includes Standards & Benchmarks

Author

Wendy Conklin, M.A.

Teacher Created Resources

Teacher Created Resources, Inc.
6421 Industry Way
Westminster, CA 92683
www.teachercreated.com

ISBN: 978-1-4206-3049-7

©*2005 Teacher Created Resources, Inc.*
Reprinted, 2010
Made in U.S.A.

Table of Contents

Teacher Lesson Plans *(cont.)*

The Activity: Day 1 (cont.)

Then pose two questions to the class: "Who invented the alphabet?" and "How was the alphabet invented?" Provide a few minutes for students to brainstorm possible ideas in their small groups. Then bring the class back together and allow each group to share two ideas.

Finally, tell the class that the questions they are trying to answer will be their mystery for this next unit of study. Distribute copies of *Graphic Organizer* (page 8). This activity is a semantic map that will show the possibilities of the invention of the alphabet. Working in their groups, students should complete this web that shows all the possibilities of the alphabet. Remind students to keep this organizer handy for use throughout this unit of study.

The Activity: Day 2

Have students form their small groups from the previous day. Distribute copies of *Background Information* (pages 9–11) for students to read in their small groups. Also provide students a copy of *A Map of the Region* (page 12) so that they can see the area of the world talked about in the background information. After every group has finished reading, take time to answer questions that students might have about the information. Remind students of Rudyard Kipling's story from the day before. How possible does this story seem now that they've read the background information? Some students might still think it is a real possibility, and others may not. There is no right or wrong answer to this question.

Take out the graphic organizers from the day before. Have students write down more possibilities on the origin of the alphabet based on what they read in the background information. Remind students to keep this organizer handy for use throughout this unit of study.

The Activity: Day 3

Provide each group with another copy of the background information from the previous day. Distribute copies of *A Timeline of the Alphabet* (page 13). Have students work in their groups to fill out the information on the timeline. This page will help students organize the time frame of theories about the invention of the alphabet. Since a timeline is not very big, remind groups to keep their notes brief but informative on these timelines.

Who Invented the Alphabet?

Teacher Lesson Plan *(cont.)*

The Activity: Day 3 *(cont.)*

Then ask students if they have ever seen the different languages described in the background information. Allow students to describe or draw what these languages look like. Tell students that you have a brief cheat sheet of information regarding how some of these languages relate to one another. Provide students with copies of *Comparison of Ancient Languages* (pages 14–15). This page compares Greek, Egyptian hieroglyphics, and ancient Semitic scripts. Have students write their name using these three languages and then compare the scripts of their name. This activity opens students' understanding that there are more languages than just English and could spark interest in further studying one of these languages. It also shows a good representation of how the languages progressed over time.

If there is any further information students would like to record on their graphic organizers, take time at the end of class for students to add to their semantic maps.

The Activity: Day 4

Tell students that they will be making a decision today about the first alphabet. Remind students that even though the latest archaeological evidence says it originated in Egypt, this is not necessarily the answer—but it could be. In the early '90s, archaeologists thought it could be the Semitic writing. Only time and further excavations will tell for sure.

Begin by having students review their graphic organizers. What do they think about the origins of the alphabet, and why do they think that? Have students gather in their groups from the previous day to discuss their opinions.

Then tell students they will be creating a story about how the alphabet came to be. This story should explain their personal position on this mystery, but can be told in a creative manner with fictional characters. Distribute copies of *The True Story of the Alphabet* (page 16). Give students the rest of the class time to complete their stories on this page.

The Activity: Day 5

Tell students that they will be sharing their stories with the class today. Have students form their groups once again. They can read their stories in their groups. Then have each group select at least one to share with the entire class. If time permits, and there are more students who want to share, allow each student to share their story. Challenge students to keep their ears open for further information on the alphabet in the future.

Attention Grabber

The following is a retelling of "How the Alphabet Was Invented" by Rudyard Kipling:

Long ago, people didn't have an alphabet or written words. They told each other stuff using drawn pictures. Sometimes people confused the pictures with one another. Some people were not very talented at drawing. One day, a cave girl and her dad decided they would create a system of symbols that everyone could understand. The cave girl's name was Tafi-rafi-googlie-amada-furgio, but most people called her Taffy; and the dad's name was Tegumai.

You might be wondering how Taffy invented the alphabet. She asked her dad to make a sound. He decided to make the sound, "ay." He looked pretty funny when he made that sound. Taffy asked him to make the sound again and hold it for a long time. She noticed that his mouth looked like the mouth of a carp that she caught in the creek.

She decided that the mouth of a carp would represent the "ay" sound, and therefore the letter A. She opened her mouth and made the "ay" sound while looking at her reflection in the water. You might be wondering how that looks like the letter A. Well, if a carp is hung upside down with its mouth open and a line is drawn across the mouth, then it looks like an A.

She asked her dad to make another sound. He made the "sssss" sound. Taffy thought it sounded like a snake. So, she drew a snake crawling around on the ground. It looked like this: S.

She continued with the other letters of the alphabet until each distinct sound had a letter to represent it and in this way, Taffy had invented the alphabet!

Graphic Organizer

Directions: Use this page to map all the possible ideas of how the alphabet originated. You will be referring back to this page throughout the course of study.

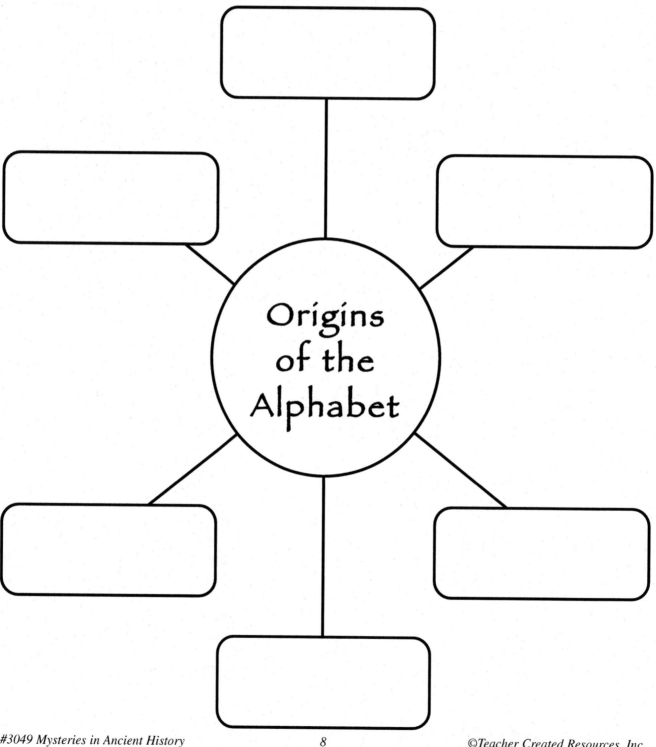

Origins
of the
Alphabet

Who Invented the Alphabet?

Background Information

Have you ever thought of the importance of the alphabet? Why do people need an alphabet? Is it possible for people to communicate without it? Without it, we could not form words using letters. It would be difficult to communicate in writing. People would have to write in pictures instead of words. It would be difficult to send e-mails and instant messages. There would be no English class in school, because without an alphabet, there would be no written words. Without written words, there would be no sentences or structure. Instead, there would be some sort of cuneiform or hieroglyphics course.

Where did the very first alphabet come from? Who invented it, and what made them see the need for an alphabet? The word *alphabet* comes from the first two Greek letters: *alpha* and *beta*. Based on this information, many people assume the alphabet came from the ancient Greeks—but is that true? Many believe it existed before the Greeks.

Many questions remain that might unlock this mystery. If the Greeks did not invent the alphabet, where did they get their alphabet? When did it show up in Greece? How did they think of adding letters to stand for consonants and vowels? And who thought up the whole idea of an alphabet in the first place? Was it one person or many who contributed to the idea of an alphabet? Or did a brilliant Egyptian get up one day and think about the need for an alphabet and suddenly scribble it down? Did it come from Mesopotamia's cuneiform or Egypt's hieroglyphics? Another form of writing existed on the island of Crete. Scholars call it Linear A and B. Were any of these three languages the inspiration for an alphabet?

Most think that the alphabet originated from the need to communicate for trade and business. But there is no evidence of business transactions in early Greek writing. Others believe the alphabet originated to record Homer's poems. If that were true, the alphabet would have originated around 800 B.C.

Others believe that children living in Canaan, located in northern Syria, invented the alphabet. Children do amazing things! Maybe these children were tired of learning cuneiform. They saw their neighbors, the Egyptians, using symbols for some of their consonant sounds in their hieroglyphics and decided to copy them. Using this information, they invented their own signs for consonants found in their spoken language.

more to follow

Background Information *(cont.)*

Rudyard Kipling, a famous writer, wrote a book called *How the Alphabet Was Made*. In his story, a little girl invented the alphabet using what she called "noise pictures." Each letter invented came from a noise. She saw her father saying, "oh" and noticed the shape of his mouth. It looked like this O. The letter S sounded like the hissing of a snake and therefore took on the shape of a snake. In this way, the girl wrote the entire alphabet. Did Kipling know something that no one else knew? Probably not.

In 1905, an archaeologist was digging in a turquoise mine in the area of the Sinai Desert. He found a sphinx that dated back to 1500 B.C. On this sphinx were some mysterious inscriptions. Beside these inscriptions were some Egyptian hieroglyphics.

When translated, the hieroglyphics said "beloved of Hathor, mistress of turquoise." Around the sphinx, the archaeologist found rocks with other inscriptions. He wondered if the mysterious script was an alphabet, because it had less than 30 signs. He knew that at one time the Hebrew (Semitic) people from Canaan had been slaves and had worked in these turquoise mines, so these mysterious signs were named "proto-Sinaitic" signs because they were found in the Sinai Desert. Could these miners in Sinai have created the first alphabet? Many people tend to doubt it, because they were just slaves and miners, not educated scribes—but no one knows for sure.

Ten years later, another archaeologist, Sir Alan Gardiner, compared these signs with some Egyptian hieroglyphics. He noticed that some of these signs were similar to the hieroglyphics and believed that they represented the same thing. He believed that the messages on the sphinx were bilingual—that is, they were written in two languages: Egyptian and Semitic. He first connected the signs with the similar-looking hieroglyphics. Then he gave each hieroglyphic a Semitic name (which is known from studying ancient texts in the Torah). What he found was the names of the letters found in the Hebrew alphabet.

more to follow

Background Information *(cont.)*

Some believed that this was too much of a stretch, but Gardiner translated one of the mysterious inscriptions using this method. Unfortunately, he could translate only one word, and it meant Baalat, or "the Lady," which was the Semitic name for a goddess named Hathor. Other inscriptions could not be translated because there is not a hieroglyphic for every sign. Is this a missing link between the early alphabet and Egyptian hieroglyphics? If so, the Egyptians may have invented the alphabet.

More recently some inscriptions have been found dating from the 16th and 17th centuries B.C. in Israel and Lebanon. Those living in this area were at the crossroads of the Babylonian, Egyptian, Hittite, and Cretan empires. It was a perfect place for a trader to be. These traders could have invented an easy-to-learn script to record their transactions with other traders. An alphabet would be easy to write, too. It seems that these sophisticated traders could have been the originators of the alphabet, but this has not been proven.

New discoveries in 1999 in Egypt include a table written by a traveling scribe. This scribe wrote letters that are similar to the Egyptian script which date back to 1900–1800 B.C. If no other ancient texts are found, then this evidence suggests that the Egyptians are the inventors of the alphabet. But this fact is not yet known for sure, and only time will solve the mystery of the alphabet.

A Map of the Region

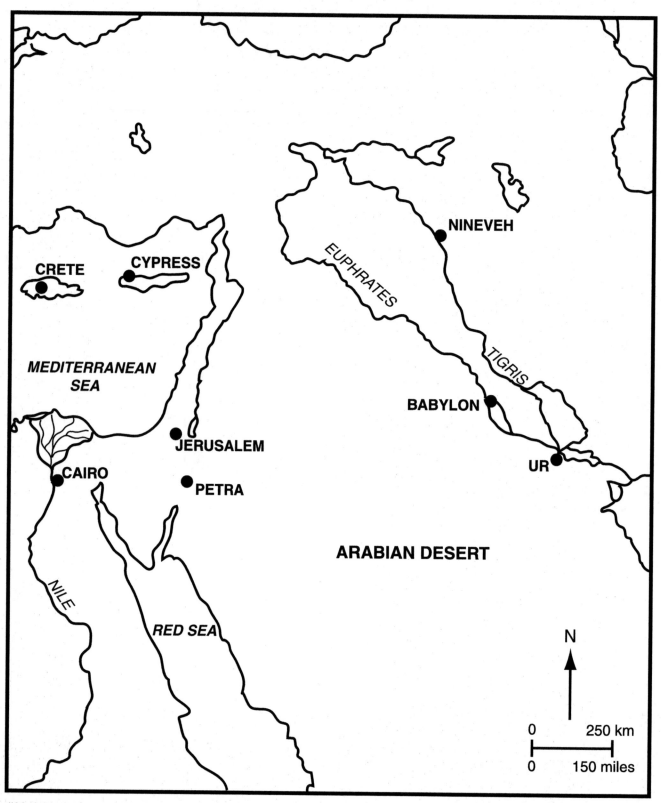

A Timeline of the Alphabet

Directions: Use the timeline on this page to keep track of the timeline of events in dating the alphabet.

Year   **Event**

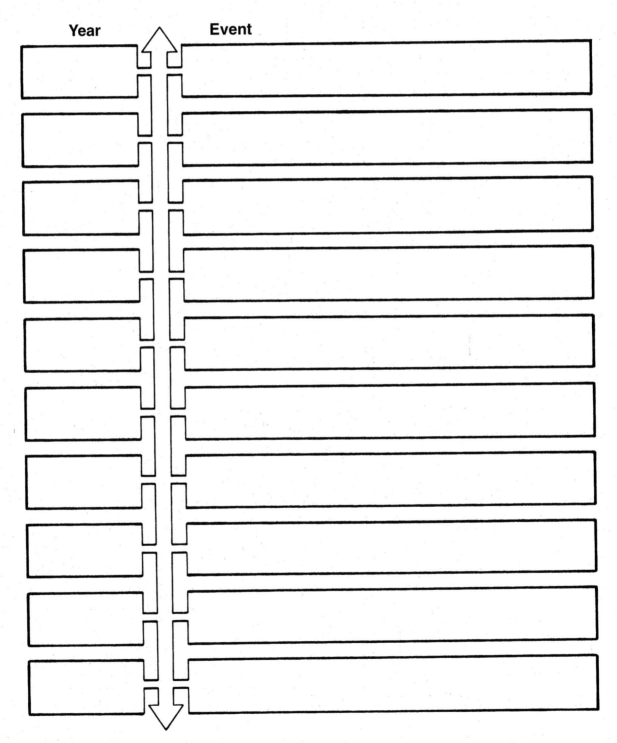

Comparison of Ancient Languages

Greek Letters

Uppercase	Lowercase	English name
A	α	alpha
B	β	beta
Γ	γ	gamma
Δ	δ	delta
E	ε	epsilon
Z	ζ	zeta
H	η	eta
Θ	θ	theta
I	ι	iota
K	κ	kappa
Λ	λ	lambda
M	μ	mu
N	ν	nu
Ξ	ξ	xi
O	o	omicron
Π	π	pi
P	ρ	rho
Σ	σ	sigma
T	τ	tau
Υ	υ	upsilon
Φ	φ	phi
X	χ	chi
Ψ	ψ	psi
Ω	ω	omega

Semitic Signs

Letter Name	Letter	Early
Aleph	A	
Beyt	B	
Gimel	G	
Dalet	D	
Hey	H	
Vav	W	
Zayin	Z	
Chet	Hh	
Tet	Th	
Yud	Y	
Kaph	K	
Lamed	L	
Mem	M	
Nun	N	
Samech	S	
Ayin	Gh	
Pey	P	
Tsade	Ts	
Quph	Q	
Resh	R	
Shin	Sh	
Tav	T	

Comparison of Ancient Languages *(cont.)*

Egyptian Hieroglyphics

A	A	B	C/K	D
eagle	arm	foot	basket	hand
E/I/Y	**F/V**	**G**	**H**	**H**
two strokes	viper	jar	house	flax
I/Y/E	**J**	**L**	**M**	**M**
seed	cobra	lion	owl	bar
N	**N**	**O/U/W**	**P**	**Q**
water	crown	lasso	door	slope
R	**S/Z**	**SH/CH**	**T**	**TH**
mouth	cloth	pool	loaf	rope
U/W/O	**X**	**Y/E/I**	**Z/S**	
chick	basket/cloth	double reed	bolt	

The True Story of the Alphabet

Directions: You have read and looked at different languages. In the space below, write your story of how you believe the alphabet came to be.

_____

_____

_____

_____

_____

_____

_____

_____

_____

_____

_____

_____

_____

_____

_____

_____

_____

Was King Tut Murdered?

Teacher Lesson Plans

Standard/Objective

✻ Identify and use processes important to reconstructing and reinterpreting the past, such as using a variety of sources; providing, validating, and weighing evidence for claims; checking credibility of sources, and searching for causality. (NCSS)

✻ Students will gather evidence about the mysterious deaths in ancient Egypt while playing a game and then decide on a theory concerning these deaths.

Materials

copies of *Attention Grabber* (page 20); copies of *Background Information* (pages 21–23); copies of *Graphic Organizer* (page 24); copies of *Evidence Cards* (pages 25–28); copies of *The Evidence Game* (page 29); copies of *A Tomb Wall Tells It All* (page 30); game markers; dice

Discussion Questions

✻ Explain what you think this letter is about.

✻ Who wrote this letter?

✻ Why did she write this letter?

✻ What seems suspicious about this letter?

✻ Do you think a famous pharaoh could have possibly been murdered?

The Activity: Day 1

Make copies of *Attention Grabber* (page 20) and address one to every student. Have students read the letter as though it was meant for them. Ask the discussion questions above. Then explain that they will be investigating the possibility of three murders in ancient Egypt. These supposed murders occurred 3,000 years ago.

Next, group students together to read *Background Information* (pages 21–23). Let them discuss this information in their small groups and make a list of any questions that still remain unanswered. Tell students that they will be deciding if these three deaths were a result of a serial killer, or many killers, or simply caused by nature. Be sure to stress that any of these deaths might not be murders at all.

Teacher Lesson Plans *(cont.)*

The Activity: Day 1 (cont.)

Make a copy of *Graphic Organizer* (page 24) for students. (Each day, a new copy of this sheet should be given to each student. All of these must be stapled together so that students can look back at how their opinion changes with each new piece of evidence.) Explain to students that they will be keeping a record of what they think about the evidence in the King Tut case. Have students record any outstanding evidence on this sheet under the appropriate title and explain why they feel one, all, or more than one is guilty of the murders. Then divide the class in half. Label one side "Aye" and the other side "Horemheb." Tell students to walk to the side of the room that represents who they believe murderered Tut. Students who walk to the middle of the room believe that his wife, Ankhesenamun, murdered Tut. Then have students do the same for the question of the death of the Hittite prince. Repeat the same activity for the death of Ankhesenamun. If students do not believe any of these suspects committed the murder or that these deaths were not murder at all, instruct them to sit down.

The Activity: Day 2

Tell students that they will gather evidence by playing a game. Have students form groups of four or five to play this game. Give each group one game board (page 29) and one set of the evidence cards (pages 25–28). Have each student select a marker for his or her game board. Some might use a penny or an eraser. Each group will also need a die to roll. First, have each player roll the die to determine the order of each player's turn. Then each player will roll the die at his or her turn and advance along the game board. When a player reaches a labeled place on the game board, he or she can choose to read an evidence card or roll again. If a player turns over a card that he or she has already read, he or she may choose the next card in the pile to read. Only one card can be read at each location. Then the player must move on to another location. He or she can return back to that location after visiting another and gathering more evidence. Some places have more evidence than others. Give students about 20 or 30 minutes to play the game.

Then distribute another copy of *Graphic Organizer* (page 24). Have students record their new evidence on this page and then decide each suspect's guilt or innocence. Let students staple this page to the one from the previous day. Then divide the class in half. Label one side "Aye" and the other side "Horemheb." Tell students to walk to the side of the room that represents who they believe murdered Tut. Students who walk to the middle of the room believe that Tut's wife, Ankhesenamun, murdered him. Then have students do the same for the question of the death of the Hittite prince. Repeat the same activity for the death of Ankhesenamun. If students do not believe any of these suspects committed the murder or that these deaths were not murder at all, instruct them to sit down.

Teacher Lesson Plans *(cont.)*

The Activity: Days 3 and 4

Allow students to continue to play the game and gather more evidence. Then distribute another copy of *Graphic Organizer* (page 24) to each student. Have students record their new evidence on this page

and then decide each suspect's guilt or innocence. Then they should staple this page to the others from the previous days.

Next, divide the class in half again. Label one side "Aye" and the other side "Horemheb." Tell students to walk to the side of the room that represents who they believe about murdered Tut. Students who walk to the middle of the room believe that Tut's wife, Ankhesenamun, murdered him. Then have students do the same for the question of the death of the Hittite prince. Repeat the same activity for the death of Ankhesenamun. If students do not believe any of these suspects committed the murder or that these deaths were not murder at all, instruct them to sit down.

Day 4 will be the last day of playing the game. No more evidence can be collected after this day.

The Activity: Day 5

Students will be making their decisions about the three deaths on this day. Distribute copies of *A Tomb Wall Tells It All* (page 30). Have students draw their conclusion to this mystery on this page as if it were a wall in an Egyptian tomb. Allow enough time for students to present this drawing at the end of class. During this time, let students ask additional questions and discuss why they made their final conclusions about this case.

Attention Grabber

My husband is dead. I do not have any sons. But you have many sons. Please send me a son to marry and he will become my husband and will be king of Egypt. I would never marry one of my servants and make him king. I am afraid!

Sincerely,

The King's Wife

Background Information

In 1922, a man named Howard Carter uncovered one of the greatest archaeological treasures: he found the tomb of King Tutankhamen, a boy king, almost completely in tact. Carter found over 2,000 objects in the four chambers, including the king's coffin, which was made from 22 lbs. of solid gold. Inside the coffin was Tut's body, and scientists concluded from it that he died very young. There are many speculations on how he died, so it is not known for sure if he was murdered, died of a sudden sickness, or died of some sort of accident.

The fact that he died so young and so suddenly have made some suspicious. The very first autopsy was performed in 1925. The doctor performing the autopsy noticed a cut on the left cheek but was unable to find a solution to his cause of death. In 1968, another doctor x-rayed Tut's body. The x-ray showed that Tut did not die of tuberculosis. It also showed that the front ribcage was missing. No other strange injuries were present on that part of the body. Because his arms were crossed over that area, some think it might have been another type of embalming method. But the x-ray did show a mysterious fragment of bone within the skull and a defect that could be a hemorrhage caused by a blow to the head. More recently, CAT scans have been performed in hoping to gain more information into his death. Although not conclusive, these scans imply that he did not die of this injury. Some now believe he was poisoned. Future tests on his organs might be able to provide some proof for this theory. Others believe he might have died from an infection brought on by a badly broken leg.

Most events surrounding King Tut's life are a mystery. Records show that King Tut ruled Egypt from 1333–1323 B.C. He inherited the throne around age 10. Many estimate that he died around age 20. It is believed he was the son of the heretic pharaoh Akhenaten. Akhenaten was known for abolishing the worship of many gods in favor of just one, the sun god, Aten. When Akhenaten died, King Tut rose to the throne. High officials—one the highest deputy army general, Horemheb; the other his chief advisor, Aye—protected him. Tut married Nefertiti's daughter, Ankhesenamun, who had been his childhood friend. Under these generals, King Tut officially returned Egypt to the worship of many gods and also restored many of the temples for worship.

Background Information *(cont.)*

Of particular interest are the paintings on the walls of the tomb. There was only one room that was painted. Most believe that is the case because there was so little time to prepare for the burial. Egyptians believed that the paintings had some sort of power. If a scene were painted, it would happen. It was a magical principle. One scene painted on the wall in the tomb shows his chief advisor, Aye, administering the funeral rites. It is very clear that he is the one performing the rites, because his name is written above his head. This type of painting was common in private tombs, but it was never seen before in a royal tomb.

After her husband's death, Queen Ankhesenamun sent a letter to the King of the Hittites (located in modern-day Turkey). The Hittites had a strong army and were regarded as Egypt's enemy. In the letter Ankhesenamun tells the king that her husband is dead. She says that she does not wish to marry one of her subjects but would rather marry a Hittite prince and make him king of Egypt. She also says that she is afraid. When the Hittite king received the letter, he could not believe it. Why would she ask her enemy for help? The offer seemed almost too good to be true. He sent a messenger to check out the offer. The Hittite king was satisfied that his son would be safe and sent a prince to marry her, along with a large entourage. But as the prince came to the Egyptian border, he was killed. Who could have murdered this prince? He was most likely protected by his bodyguards. When the Hittite king found out, he became very angry and went to war with Egypt.

What happened to Ankhesenamun? A ring surfaced in the 1930s in Egypt that told the story. On the ring was inscribed the cartouche of Aye and the cartouche of Ankhesenamun. The union of both of these cartouches means that they married. Tut's chief advisor Aye married Ankhesenamun, and he became king of Egypt.

Even more mysterious is Ankhesenamun's disappearance soon after the marriage. One thing we do know: she disappeared without a trace. Her tomb is nowhere to be found, and her name is virtually erased from Egyptian history. Even if her tomb were plundered, there would still be some trace of her name in the tomb.

more to follow

Background Information *(cont.)*

It is also important to note that Aye already had a wife, Tey. She was the queen painted on the walls of Aye's tomb, and she was given the label of "the great wife." Aye was in his 60s when he became king of Egypt. He had been married to the same woman for more than 40 years. Aye was also a faithful employee of both King Tut's and Akhenaten's reign. He attended to the burial of Tut with care, and many believe he truly loved his young master.

Aye only ruled for four years before dying. Robbers raided his tomb, but there seems to have been a desecration of his tomb even before the robbers took hold. His name was erased from the monuments inside his tomb. This name-erasing was not uncommon in Egypt. If someone wanted another not to fare well in the afterlife, they erased the name. The servant statues were also completely destroyed. Horemheb succeeded as king after Aye's death. It was most likely Horemheb who destroyed Aye's tomb. Horemheb also destroyed Tut's name on many of the monuments and had his own name put in its place. That is also why Tut's history is so difficult to piece together. In fact, Horemheb had Akhenaten's, Tut's, and Aye's names erased from every monument or document, as though they never existed. He took credit for their reign. He also restored order to the courts in Egypt, admonishing the judges to not take bribes. Criminals were strictly punished. Temples and shrines were built, and he restored greatness to the land.

The mysteries in Egypt during this time include two deaths and one disappearance. The death of the Hittite prince was certainly murder. The death of Tutankhamen is suspicious, at the very least; and the disappearance of Queen Ankhesnamun causes one to wonder if there were three murders instead of just one. All three added together makes for a pretty interesting story—maybe even a conspiracy to control the throne.

Graphic Organizer

Directions: Use the organizer below to keep track of your notes in the case.

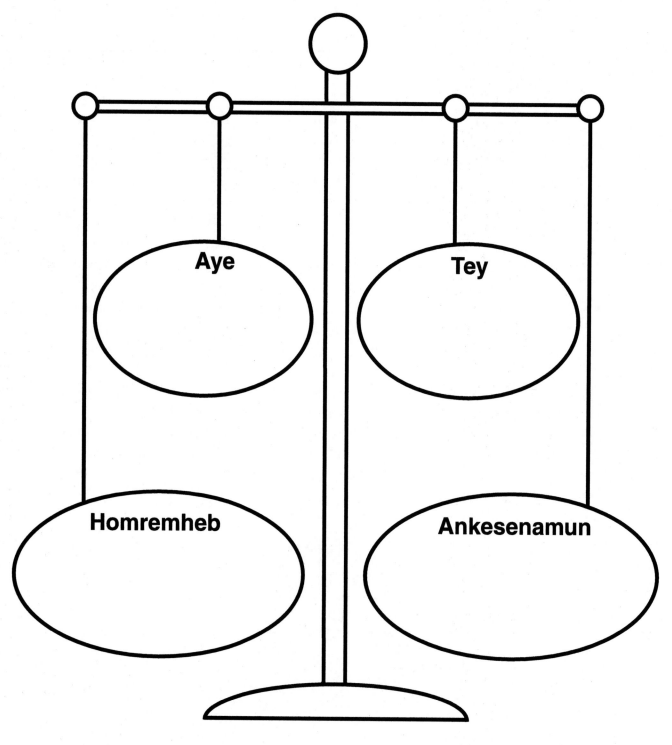

Aye

Tey

Homremheb

Ankesenamun

Evidence Cards

King Tut Some speculate that as Tut grew older, his views might have changed. He might have begun to exert his power over those who had once controlled him. Would this have sat well with his two main advisors?	***King Tut*** Many other artifacts in Tut's tomb suggest that they were not meant for him.
King Tut King Tut and his wife Ankhesenamun did not have any children.	***King Tut*** However, Tut was young and was not prepared to die, like an old pharaoh would have been. So a tomb would not have been ready.
King Tut Tut was the last of the bloodline of his family. Whoever married his wife would surely be king.	***King Tut*** Tut might have died of a plague that was causing many deaths in Egypt.
King Tut Another reason for suspicion regarding Tut's death was the hurried burial.	***Aye*** Some think this indicates that Aye had to justify his rise to the throne in light of the events surrounding the king's death. So he had his picture painted on Tut's wall.
King Tut The wooden coffin was made for another king but was used for Tut instead.	***Aye*** Aye arranged for the wall to be painted with himself (as king) giving the last rites.

Evidence Cards *(cont.)*

Aye

Aye did not allow his future young wife to be painted on the walls of Tut's tomb, though this was the custom.

Aye

Some believe Aye was merely putting on a show for his subjects as he cared for Tut's tomb.

Aye

In the picture on the wall of the tomb, Aye is wearing a crown, suggesting that he is the rightful heir to the throne. This is very unusual in Egyptian art.

Aye

When Aye took the throne, he had no children to succeed him.

Aye

Aye would not have wanted to have a Hittite king. He knew the Hittite prince would appoint his own advisors— and so Aye would be out of a job.

Tey

Tey had already held a place of prominence in the Egyptian society as Nefertiti's confidant.

Aye

It had to be someone with the military power to order the murder of the Hittite prince. Aye had the motive and the power to do this.

Tey

She might have had the motive for murdering Ankhesenamun.

Aye

Did Aye have Tut and this Hittite prince killed so that he could take the throne? Did Aye even kill his new young wife?

Was King Tut Murdered?

Evidence Cards *(cont.)*

Horemheb

Under Tut's general, Horemheb, many of the Hittite warriors were killed in battle.

Horemheb

Did Horemheb believe that he could grab the throne when Aye died four years later?

Horemheb

Certainly Horemheb would not have wanted his enemy to rule over Egypt.

Horemheb

His power as general and the backing of his powerful army made sure he could take the throne upon Aye's death.

Horemheb

It had to be someone with the military power to order the murder of the Hittite prince. Horemheb had the motive and the power as general to do this.

Tey

Tey certainly would not have taken a back seat to another younger wife.

Horemheb

He did many great things for Egypt— but does all this mean that he is innocent of murder?

Ankhesenamun

In her letter, Ankhesenamun doesn't name any names but she does imply that she is being forced to marry a servant.

Horemheb

Horemheb certainly did not want Aye to keep the younger Ankhesenamun as his wife. She was young enough to have children who would ascend the throne.

Evidence Cards *(cont.)*

Ankhesenamun

She might have been
forced into the marriage.

Ankhesenamun

One of two things is sure: either her tomb
has not yet been found, or she was not
given a proper burial.

Ankhesenamun

Her desperate letter seems to conclude
the she did not want to marry her servant.
Was Ankhesenamun referring to Aye as the
servant she didn't want to marry?

Ankhesenamun

Was Ankhesenamun simply punished
for offering the throne to a foreigner
(something considered treasonous)?

Ankhesenamun

Another interesting clue is found on the walls
of Tut's tomb. It was common to include a
picture of the queen on the wall of her husband's
tomb so that she would spend eternity with him.
She was not painted on the walls of Tut's tomb.

Ankhesenamun

Could the murderer of Tut be Ankhesenamun?
Maybe she wanted to rule Egypt
herself through a foreigner?

Ankhesenamun

Nor was she on the walls of Aye's tomb.
Was her disappearance foul play
by a murderer?

Ankhesenamun

The Hittites had a powerful military
and would definitely back her up, if needed.

Ankhesenamun

Or did Ankhesenamun die of a plague
that was consuming Egypt at the time?

Ankhesenamun

If Ankhesenamun killed Tut, Aye would
be seen as the defender of Egypt's liberty
against a scheming queen who
murdered her own husband.

The Evidence Game

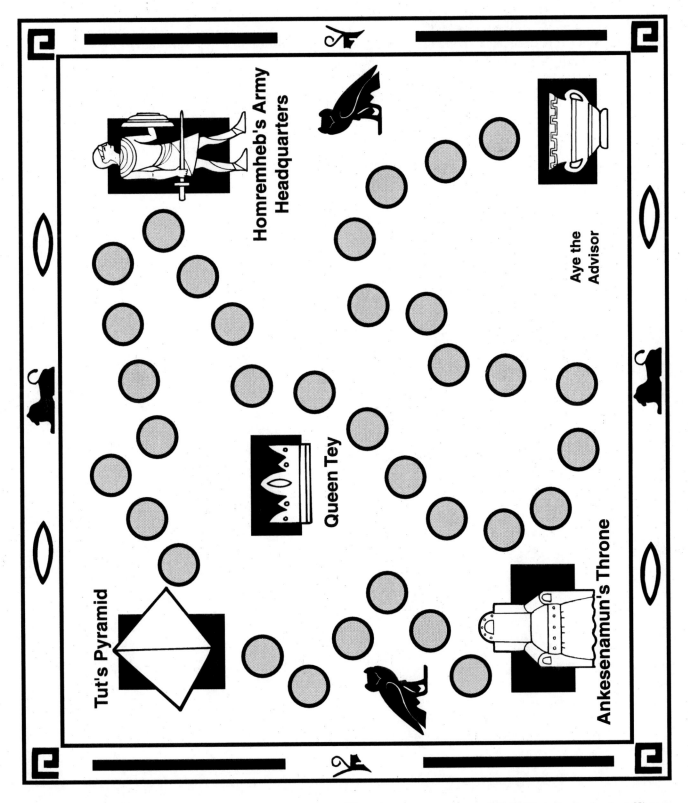

A Tomb Wall Tells It All

Directions: What is your explanations of these mysterious deaths? Are they truly mysterious, or were they the result of natural causes? Imagine this paper was a wall in an Egyptian tomb. Draw your conclusion to this three-fold mystery.

Troy: Was there a Horse?

Teacher Lesson Plans

Standard/Objective

✻ Explain how language, literature, the arts, architecture, artifacts, traditions, beliefs, values, and behaviors contribute to the development and transmission of culture. (NCSS)

✻ Students will hear Homer's story, analyze an ancient piece of artwork, and read about archaeological findings and then write their own play showing whether or not there was a Trojan horse.

Materials

copies of *Attention Grabber* (page 33); copies of *The Rest of the Story* (page 34); copies of *Laocoön's Hunch* (pages 35–36); copies of *Graphic Organizer* (page 37); copies of *Background Information* (pages 38–40); copies of *Finding Troy* (page 41); copies of *Did the Trojan Horse Exist?* (page 42); copies of *The True Story of Troy* (page 43)

Discussion Questions

✻ Do you think that this play could be based on a true story?

✻ For what reasons do you think this could be true?

✻ For what reasons do you think this is not a true story?

✻ What advice would you give the Trojans regarding the horse?

✻ What do you think the Trojans will do with the horse?

The Activity: Day 1

To get students excited about this topic, they will be reading a play about the events that took place in Homer's Troy. Make copies of the first page of *Attention Grabber* (page 33). (Note: Be sure to copy only page 33. Students will read the second and third pages of the play the following day.) There are 12 parts in this play. Assign students parts and have them read it. If you have 24 or more students, divide the class in half and have them read the play in two different groups. Then ask the discussion questions above.

Ask students to think silently about what they think happens next in the story. Distribute copies of *The Rest of the Story* (page 34). On this page students will be writing the rest of the play to show what they think happens next in the story. Give students between 10 and 15 minutes to complete the play with their own versions. Then have them break into small groups (3 or 4 per group) and share their plays, having the others in the group read the parts as before.

After everyone has finished sharing their plays, explain to students that they will find out what happens in the play the following day.

Teacher Lesson Plans (cont.)

The Activity: Day 2

Begin class by having students read *The Conclusion of "Laocoön's Hunch"* (pages 35–36). Have students read the same parts as they read the day before. (Note: some of the speaking parts were not on the first page of the play.) Provide a few moments for students to share how this ending was different from the ending that they wrote the previous day. Tell students that the mystery they will be discussing is the possibility of the Trojan horse. Explain that this story comes from two very famous poems, called *The Iliad* and *The Odyssey,* written by a man named Homer. Some think that what Homer wrote was actual history.

Distribute copies of *Graphic Organizer* (page 37). Students will be keeping track of this debate on this page. Tell students to keep this organizer handy for the remainder of the week to record information that will help them to decide whether there really was a Trojan horse.

The Activity: Day 3

Begin by reminding students of the story about the Trojan horse. Distribute copies of *Background Information* (pages 38–40). Divide students into small groups (3 or 4 to a group) and have them read this information in these small groups. After all the groups have finished reading, take a few moments for students to voice their questions. Then have students take out their graphic organizers. Have students write any information that they believe will help them prove or disprove the reality of the Trojan horse. Have students share their information in their small groups again. At this time, students may add additional information to their graphic organizers to help them differentiate the information. Remind students to keep these graphic organizers to record information on the following day.

The Activity: Day 4

Distribute copies of *Finding Troy* (page 41). This sheet will help students understand where Troy was located in ancient times. Have students consult maps and globes to fill in the information.

Then distribute copies of *Did the Trojan Horse Exist?* (page 42). This activity sheet has an ancient drawing of a battering ram. Read the directions together and then have students analyze the picture. In small groups (3 or 4 to a group), students can discuss what they think about the battering ram and the horse in Homer's poem. Then have students record their information on their graphic organizers.

The Activity: Day 5

Begin by telling the class that it is time for them to make their final decisions about the Trojan horse. Have them look back at their graphic organizers for help. Then distribute copies of *The True Story of Troy* (page 43). Read the directions together. Then allow time for students to write their play.

Divide students into small groups (3 or 4 per group) and have them read their plays aloud. If time permits, let each group choose one to present to the class. Take these plays and copy and bind them for the entire class to enjoy. If possible, provide the library and office with a copy so that others can read about their well-researched conclusions.

Attention Grabber

"Laocoön's Hunch"

Cast of Characters

Laocoön	Sinon	Cassandra, the king's daughter
Trojan 1, 2, 3	Sea serpent 1, 2	Greek 1, 2
Priam, King of Troy	children	

Trojan 1: This war has gone on too long now! Has it really been 10 years?

Trojan 2: And it all started over our king's son, Paris, taking the most beautiful woman, Helen, away from her husband in Greece.

Trojan 3: Yes, Paris just had to have her!

Trojan 1: I'm surprised that her Greek husband has fought this long for her.

Trojan 2: Don't forget all those Greeks who swore to protect her marriage to him! That's why this war is not over yet!

Trojan 3: You are right! Her husband couldn't fight this war alone. But maybe he wants to kill her for betraying him?

Priam: Look there in the distance. What is that I see? Are the black ships leaving us?

Trojan 1: Yes! Let's go down to the shore and make sure.

Priam: Don't forget your armor and weapons. Those Greeks might be trying to trap us.

Trojan 2: I'll go down to scout out the area first.

Trojan 3: Well, those Greeks have gone, but they've left something behind.

Priam: Look at that beautiful horse!

Trojan 1: It's the biggest horse I've ever seen! And the wood is gleaming!

Trojan 2: I wonder how they built that!

Trojan 3: Why would they build something like that?

Laocoön: Don't get near that horse! Don't even touch it!

Priam: Why, my dear priest, should we be alarmed? It's just a wooden horse.

Laocoön: No, it's not just a horse! Do you really think those Greeks would leave something behind that is harmless?

The Rest of the Story

Directions: Now that you've read part of the story, what do you think happens next? Write the ending of this play using at least three characters to show what happens to the Trojans. You can even choose to write yourself into the story.

_____   _____

_____   _____

_____   _____

_____   _____

_____   _____

_____   _____

_____   _____

_____   _____

_____   _____

_____   _____

_____   _____

                            _____

The Conclusion of "Laocoön's Hunch"

Trojan 1: I think you are blowing this out of proportion, Laocoön. We know you are the priest of Poseidon, the god of the sea, but do you really know anything about horses?

Trojan 2: What are you going to do with that spear, Laocoön?

Trojan 3: Now, why did you have to go and throw that spear at the helpless wooden horse?

Trojan 1: Look over here, King Priam. We have found a Greek hiding in the tall grass!

Trojan 2: Maybe if we light his feet on fire, he will tell us the secret about this wooden horse!

Priam: What is the meaning of this? Tell me your name!

Sinon: I am Sinon, and it is true that I'm a Greek. But I am a miserable Greek! Even my own people hate me.

Priam: Okay, tell us why they hate you, and then maybe we won't hate you.

Sinon: Odysseus, the Greek king of Ithaca, killed my master. I was very angry about that. I said some things I shouldn't have said out loud, and Odysseus heard me. He came after me to kill me, too. Oh, what's the use! You won't believe my story, anyway. Go ahead and kill me. Helen's husband will be glad to be rid of me!

Priam: That makes me curious about your story. I want to hear more. Go on and tell me.

Sinon: Well, the Greeks consulted the gods about going home. The gods told them to sacrifice one person to make sure the winds and the waves would be mild on their trip home.

Priam: And I suppose you were the one sacrificed?

Sinon: Yes, and they left this horse as a peace offering to Athena, the goddess of war.

Trojan 1: Well, I believe him.

Trojan 2: Yes, I think we all do.

Priam: Unbind this poor fellow and let him go free.

Trojan 3: I'm just glad to hear that this horse is not a threat to us. What a great idea to offer Athena a peace offering!

Trojan 2: What is that in the distance?

Trojan 3: It looks like two large sea serpents!

The Conclusion of "Laocoön's Hunch" *(cont.)*

Sea serpent 1: Let's get Laocoön's two children!

Sea serpent 2: Yes, they are right there on the shore and should be easy to handle.

Children: Help! The sea serpents are squeezing us! Help us, father!

Laocoön: Don't worry, children! I will save you!

Trojan 1: That's awful! Did you see those serpents destroy Laocoön's children?

Trojan 2: Look, they have Laocoön, too.

Trojan 3: They've just left him dead. This is too awful to watch.

Priam: Take this as a lesson, everyone.

Trojan 1: These serpents must have been sent by Athena to punish Laocoön for his warning.

Trojan 2: This horse was not a threat to us. It was an offering to her.

Priam: You are right, my fellow Trojans! Let's pull it into the city gates!

Cassandra: Don't bring that horse inside the city gates! It will be the end of us if you do!

Trojan 3: Oh, she doesn't know what she is talking about.

Cassandra: But I have the gift of knowing the future! Listen to me!

Trojan 1: This time she will be wrong! She didn't see what happened to Laocoön down there.

Greek 1: Well, it's finally nighttime, and the city is quiet.

Greek 2: I thought all that dancing and music would go on all night! I'm glad it's over.

Greek 1: Yes, let's get this over with!

Sinon: My fellow Greek friends! Are you still alive inside that wooden horse?

Greek 2: Yes, and we are ready to take the city of Troy by surprise! Give us just a moment to open that trap door, and we will be out!

Sinon: I just signaled the ships way out on the sea, and they are coming just as quickly as they can to help us take the city!

Greek 1: Open those city gates for our fellow warriors. It is now the end of Troy! We will defeat her once and for all!

Greek 2: And take back Helen for our king!

Graphic Organizer

There was a horse. ← | There wasn't a horse. →

Troy: Was There a Horse?

Background Information

The ancient city of Troy has mesmerized people's imagination for centuries. The fact that Troy is so well known is due to the famous poet, Homer. There is not much known about Homer except that he wrote two great epic poems, *The Iliad* and *The Odyssey*. These stories were passed down orally generation after generation for many years, but Homer finally wrote them down sometime between 800 and 700 B.C. Not much is known about Homer, though. No one knows exactly when he lived, but many think he lived sometime around 850 B.C. Many supposed that if the Trojan war did happen, it probably took place three or four hundred years earlier.

Homer's story *The Iliad* is about a 10-year war over a woman that occurred in a place called Troy. This story begins with a rivalry between Hera, Zeus's wife, and their two daughters, Aphrodite and Athena. The goddess of discord, Eris, brought a golden apple to a wedding ceremony. She told the crowd that the apple was for the fairest woman there. Hera, Aphrodite, and Athena all believed they should be given the apple. Eris wanted Zeus to decide, but Zeus declined to answer. Instead, he let Paris, the son of Priam (the king of Troy), decide. All three women promised Paris something in return for this apple: Hera promised Paris amazing power; Athena promised Paris that he would have glory on the battlefield; but Aphrodite promised Paris that he could have the love of the most beautiful earthly woman. Paris gave Aphrodite the apple.

At that time, the most beautiful woman on Earth was Helen. Unfortunately, she was already married to Menelaus, the king of Sparta. Back in Troy, Paris became the ambassador to Sparta. When he arrived in Sparta, Aphrodite caused Helen to fall in love with Paris, and they ran away to Troy. They also took much of Menelaus's riches with them. Menelaus just happened to be away on business at the time, but when he heard what had happened, he sent 1,000 ships against Troy to get Helen and his wealth back. The war lasted 10 long years. Close to the end of the war, Homer described a huge wooden horse that the Greeks left at the gate of Troy. Menelaus's army retreated, and it appeared to the people of Troy that they had given up. The Trojans believed they had won the war, so they brought the large horse into the city. At night, the Greek soldiers who were hiding inside the wooden horse came out and opened the city gates to let other fellow soldiers in. They defeated the Trojans and took Helen back to her husband.

more to follow

Troy: Was There a Horse?

Background Information *(cont.)*

For many years, most archaeologists did not believe that Troy was a real place, but rather that it was a fictional place invented by Homer. But there was one man who believed it existed, and he set out to prove it. His name was Heinrich Schliemann. Schliemann was a self-made millionaire from Germany. When he was young, he studied very hard and eventually mastered 18 foreign languages. After earning most of his wealth, he began studying archaeology and history. As a young boy, he heard the tales about many of the ancient lost cities, and Troy was one of them. He traveled to many places, including Greece and Turkey, where he believed he could find the ancient cities talked about in Homer's poems. In fact, Schliemann used *The Iliad* and *The Odyssey* as a sort of guidebook. He believed that Homer's tales were a true recording of history.

In *The Iliad*, Homer described cities and kingdoms that really existed. Some of these kingdoms formed alliances with each other and fought against others. Homer describes this, too. In addition, Homer described the kingdom of Menelaus, located in Mycenae in Greece, as a large civilization. Archaeologists today believe that this is accurate.

But when Schliemann set out to find the city of Troy, many believed it didn't exist at all. Those who did think it once existed thought it was in Turkey at a place called Bali Dagh. Schliemann took his copy of *The Iliad* and inspected the site. He didn't believe this could be the site of Troy, so he moved on to a new site called Hissarlik. Hissarlik was located on a large plateau, and it was close to the sea where long ago ancients traded their goods. Based on the size of the plateau, Schliemann also calculated the walls of the city being about three miles in circumference. In *The Iliad*, there is a chase between Hector and Achilles. Homer describes these two warriors chasing each other around the city three times, which would equal nine miles total, at the site of Hissarlik. Schliemann thought that was a reasonable distance.

Schliemann was so convinced that Hissarlik was the right site that he dug a trench right through the middle of the plateau from north to south. In the process, Schliemann destroyed much of what he found underneath. Instead of finding one ancient city, he found nine ancient cities. They were stacked on top of each other. Long ago, people built new cities right on top of old ones. Fires and earthquakes destroyed some of these cities. The oldest city dated from about 3000 B.C.

more to follow

Background Information *(cont.)*

In the process of digging this trench, he found not only altars for sacrifice and a large palace, but also a treasure. He believed this treasure to be King Priam's treasure, but time has proved that he was wrong. This treasure was actually 1,000 years older than the city of Troy that he was searching for. Archaeologists have determined that the city of Troy referred to in Homer's *Iliad* was either the sixth or the seventh level. Today, archaeologists think that level seven was burned down sometime during the 13th century. Level six was destroyed by either an earthquake or some other violent means.

After such great success at Troy, Schliemann turned to Mycenae to see if he could find the ancient Greek civilization that invaded Troy in Homer's story. He had luck there, too. It appears that they were traders and raiders throughout the Mediterranean world. Mycenae pottery was also discovered at Troy, which tends to support that the Mycenaeans were the Greeks who invaded Troy. Archaeologists also found a suit of bronze armor that belonged to the Mycenaeans, too. Homer described this armor in *The Iliad*.

If there was a war between the Greeks and Trojans, what was the exact reason for it? The Trojans may have imposed a tax on ships going through the straits. They might have wanted to stop Greek ships from passing into the Black Sea. Maybe the Greeks wanted to control the Trojans because their city was in a key location for trading. Troy was located in an ideal location for fishing and had a tremendous supply year round. Maybe the Greeks wanted that city for the fishing bay. We know that the Hittites would go to war to reclaim their own people taken away by foreign kings. Would it be possible that the Greeks would do the same?

The Hittites were a group of people who lived in Anatolia (modern-day Turkey). They have some tables that explain a kingdom near the Dardanelles. They call this kingdom Wilusa. Another name for Wilusa is Ilium and Ilium is another name for Troy. The Hittites also record information about a seafaring people with a kingdom called Ahhiyawans. The word *Ahhiyawans* is similar to the name *Achaeans*. Homer used that name in his poems. Is it possible that the Hittites recorded information about Troy and the Greeks?

Questions still remain about Troy, and they will probably never be answered with absolute certainty. Was there a war that lasted for 10 years? Or were there many wars? Since Homer appears to be very accurate in his description of Troy and the surrounding areas in his two poems, should everything in Homer's poems be taken literally? Was he merely telling history in the form of a poem so that the generations to come would know what happened at Troy? These questions and many more about the ancient city of Troy continue to be debated to this day.

Finding Troy

Directions: Label these places on the map below.

Bodies of Water	Cities/Countries
✽ Aegean Sea	✽ Greece
✽ Black Sea	✽ Sparta
✽ Dardenelles	✽ Troy
✽ Ionian Sea	✽ Turkey/Anatolia

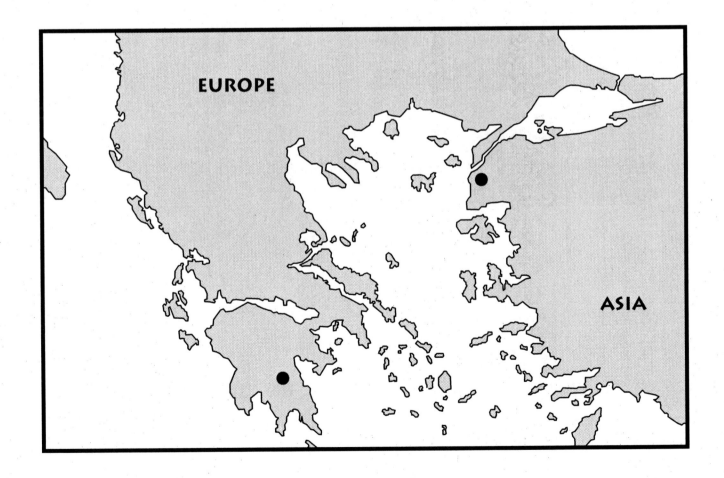

Did the Trojan Horse Exist?

In the Ancient Near East (which Troy is part of) during the 13th century, there were pictures and texts produced that talked about battering rams. Battering rams were built in the shape of horses and were used as siege engines. Armies used these battering rams to break through the enemy's city gates. Some who think the Trojan horse was a true part of Homer's story say that the poem says that the gates were broken down when the horse entered the city. In the picture below, look at the depiction of this battering ram (inside the black box).

Courtesy of British Museum

The True Story of Troy

Directions: There has been much debate in Hollywood about the Trojan horse. Broadway has advertised that they want a play titled *The True Story of Troy*. You are a well-known researcher and playwright, so you decide to submit your findings in a play. In the space below, write a section of the play in your own words that shows your opinion regarding whether or not the Trojan horse existed.

Teacher Lesson Plans

Standard/Objective

✳ Explain how language, literature, the arts, architecture, artifacts, traditions, beliefs, values, and behaviors contribute to the development and transmission of culture. (NCSS)

✳ Students will investigate the different views of who built Stonehenge and then write a magazine story about the builders and their reasons for building it.

Materials

copies of *Attention Grabber* (page 47); copies of *Graphic Organizer* (page 48); overhead of *Drawing of Stonehenge Today* (page 49); copies of *Background Information* (pages 50–52); copies of *Stonehenge Map* (page 53); copies of *Recipe for a Perfect News Story* (pages 54); copies of *A Conversation at Stonehenge* (page 55)

Discussion Questions

✳ What do you think this quote is about?

✳ Does this quote seem like fiction or nonfiction? How do you know?

✳ Who is Geoffrey of Monmouth?

✳ Are there any real monuments that this quote can describe today?

✳ How long ago do you think this was written?

The Activity: Day 1

Make several copies of *Attention Grabber* (page 47). Before students come to class, place a copy on each desk so that the students will see it. Don't provide students with any answers about it. Read it aloud as a class and ask the discussion questions above. Tell students that even when the answer to a mystery seems to be quite obvious, there could be other answers. Tell students that this quote is about the famous monument called Stonehenge.

Distribute *Graphic Organizer* (page 48) to each student. Have students write down the information that they know under the title "What I Know." Tell students to keep this graphic organizer in a safe place, because they will use it again as they record important information that they will learn.

Teacher Lesson Plans *(cont.)*

The Activity: Day 1 *(cont.)*

Place an overhead transparency of *Drawing of Stonehenge Today* (page 49) so that students can get a picture of it in their minds. Have students talk about what they see in the picture.

Then distribute copies of *Background Information* (pages 50–52) and have students read it together in small groups. Bring students back as a class and take time for students to ask and clarify questions. Then have students take out their graphic organizers again and record notes about what they have learned under the title "What I Learned."

The Activity: Day 2

Put this question on the board: "Who built Stonehenge?" Distribute copies of the *Stonehenge Map* (page 53) for students to reference. Have students look back at their notes on their graphic organizer pages. Try to get students talking about all the possibilities. Tell students that they will choose a view and write a news story about it. For example, students can choose the ancient Briton, Roman, Druid, or Greek view. This view does not necessarily have to be their personal opinion. Students should also give a reason in their articles for why Stonehenge was built.

This solution to who built Stonehenge and why will be written in a kids' news magazine. It would be helpful to bring in a copy of a news magazine so that students can get a first-hand look at the types of stories printed in it. (It should be noted that some of these magazines could have inappropriate stories, so teachers should preview the printed materials and censor some of the stories by tearing them out.) Distribute *Recipe for a Perfect News Story* (page 54). This activity sheet will help students organize their news stories. Let students spend the remaining time organizing the points of their stories.

The Activity: Day 3

Tell students that they will begin writing their stories today. Have them use information on their graphic organizers, background information, and student activity sheets to help them write. Each story should be at least one page in length and have at least one picture.

Teacher Lesson Plans *(cont.)*

The Activity: Day 4

Let students finish writing their stories. Before turning in their stories, let students share their stories with the class. These would also make a great display on a bulletin board.

Ask the following questions:

* ❋ Who had the most convincing story? What made it convincing?

* ❋ How much power does the printed material have over its readers?

* ❋ Do you think a news magazine is reliable information?

Have students take out their graphic organizers. Each student should fill in the space titled "What I Still Want to Know." Then collect each student's graphic organizer. You should also collect the student activity sheets.

The Activity: Day 5

Finally, distribute the student activity sheet *A Conversation at Stonehenge* (page 55). Students will be using this page to write their opinions about the mystery of Stonehenge. Students will be writing their opinions of Stonehenge from the Stonehenge's perspective. This activity not only makes students use higher-level thinking skills as they make judgments, they are also using their creativity as they make the monument tell the "true" story. If time permits, let students share their stories in small groups, having students read the various parts. These stories also make a great class booklet that can be copied, bound together, and then distributed to the students and the library.

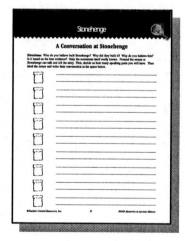

Attention Grabber

"Send for the Giants' Round which is on Mount Killarus in Ireland. For there stands a stone construction which no man of this age could ever erect, unless he combined great cunning and artistry. The stones are enormous. If they are placed round this site, in the way they are put up over there, they will stand here for ever. Many years ago the Giants transported them from the furthest ends of Africa and set them up in Ireland at a time when they lived in that country."

—Geoffrey of Monmouth

Graphic Organizer

Directions: What is the answer to the mystery of Stonehenge? Who built it, and why was it built? Under the title "What I Know," write everything you know about this monument. On the stone titled "What I Want to Know," write the questions you have. As you find out more information about Stonehenge, record your notes under the "What I Learned" title. After all your research is complete, write what else you would like to know under the title "What I Still Want to Know."

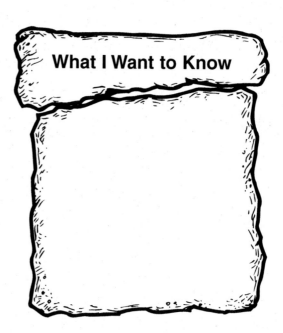

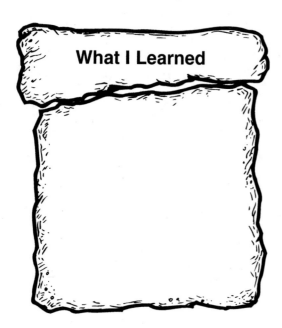

Drawing of Stonehenge Today

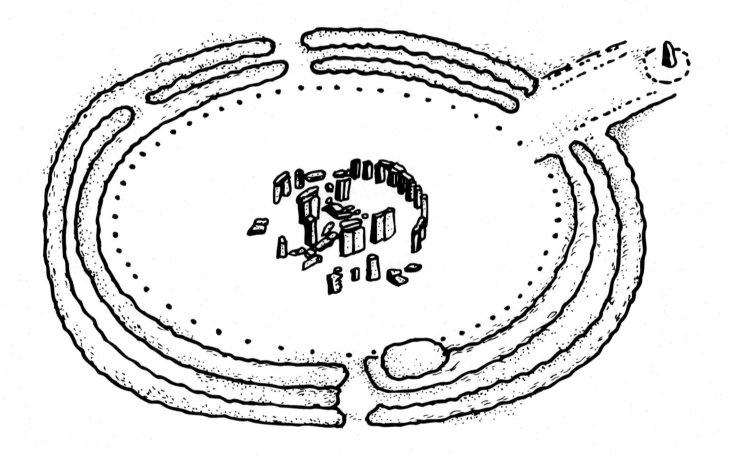

Background Information

Travelers to England hardly ever miss one of its most spectacular sites, Stonehenge. It is located on Salisbury Plain, right in between structures of modern-day highways. Some of the stones are still standing, and others have fallen down. Even before the days of radio carbon dating, archaeologists knew it was very old. They said that it was built before 1500 B.C. Today, archaeologists know that it took 2,000 years to complete it from start to finish. Who built this massive circular stone structure, and why did they build it?

Even back during medieval times people were wondering about these questions. A Welsh writer said that Stonehenge was created by Merlin, the famous wizard in the King Arthur tales. In his explanation, he said that Arthur's uncle, Aurelius Ambrosius, commissioned it. It was his way of celebrating a victory over the invading Anglo-Saxons. Merlin told Ambrosius that they should gather stones from Ireland, create the monument, and have the monument floated to Britain. Merlin said that these stones should be used because they had magical powers.

King James I, who lived during Shakespeare's time, also wondered about Stonehenge. He sent his court architect to find out about it. His architect concluded that the Romans built it for one of their Roman gods—but the Romans did not arrive in Britain until 100 B.C.

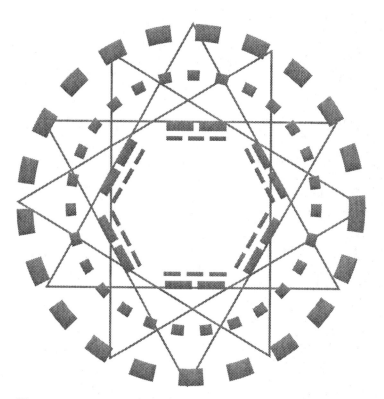

Background Information *(cont.)*

For years others had tried to credit Stonehenge to the Celtic priests called Druids. But the Druids did not arrive before 500 B.C. Others said the Danes or the Anglo-Saxons built it. In fact, it was credited to almost anyone other than the ancient Britons. But the radio carbon dating has confirmed that it was built long before any of these groups were in Britain. So, it is known that they did not build Stonehenge.

In 1953, an archaeologist named Richard Atkinson was inspecting the site and taking pictures. He was especially interested in some 17th-century graffiti. When he looked through his camera to photograph this, he noticed some other carvings that had been previously overlooked. He saw a dagger that pointed to the ground and four axes. These axes were the type found in England during the time of Stonehenge's creation. The dagger, however, was not something common in England during that time. It was the sort of dagger found in ancient Greece. In fact, it was similar to the daggers found in the royal graves located in Mycenae, Greece. And the daggers in Greece dated back to 1500 B.C. For a while it seemed as if the archaeologist had a big clue to this mystery. Atkinson believed that Stonehenge was designed and built by a visiting architect from the Mediterranean area near Greece. He even speculated that a Mycenaean prince might be buried at the site.

In the 1960s, a new form of radio carbon dating was invented, and Stonehenge was put to the test again. It revealed that the building at Stonehenge began sometime around 2950 B.C. Scientists were faced with the reality that the primitive people who lived near Salisbury Plain were the lone builders of Stonehenge. Something even more amazing was the fact that these people gathered at least 85 stones from 150 miles away. The stones used are called bluestones, and they are from the Preseli Mountains located in southwestern Wales.

Some of these stones weigh five tons each, so archaeologists began to wonder how the people moved them to Salisbury Plain. To answer this question, archaeologists took another look at the Merlin story. They thought there might be some answers in this story that was passed down in the oral tradition. In the story, the stones were floated to Salisbury Plain. Archaeologists wondered if the stones were shipped to Salisbury Plain in the same way.

more to follow

Background Information *(cont.)*

Archaeologists also wondered why the people of Stonehenge went so far to get the stones to build. There were other kinds of stones nearby, so why weren't they used instead? To answer this question, some looked again to the Merlin story. Maybe the people believed that the stones from the mountains in Wales had magical powers. Somehow they managed to ship these stones and get them to Salisbury Plain.

Astronomers made some amazing claims about Stonehenge, too. In the 18th century, an astronomer noted that Stonehenge was aligned with the rising of the sun, especially during the solstices. Others believed it was aligned with the moon and stars, as well. In the 1960s, an astronomer argued that the circle of pits around Stonehenge known as Aubrey Holes were used by the ancients to predict eclipses of the moon. But archaeologists showed evidence that these pits were used for cremations at one time and then were covered up. They argued against the lunar eclipse idea completely. Some astronomers believed Stonehenge was built to be an observatory. One astronomer said that there were 165 key points in Stonehenge that correlated with the sun. Others provide arguments to the contrary.

Over the past few years, archaeologists and astronomers have found common ground to agree. They have concluded that there are a few celestial alignments regarding the sun with Stonehenge. Many think that these alignments cannot be merely a coincidence. So, the question remains: why did the ancient builders of Stonehenge create it? Was it used as an observatory, for sacred rituals, or for something else?

Stonehenge Map

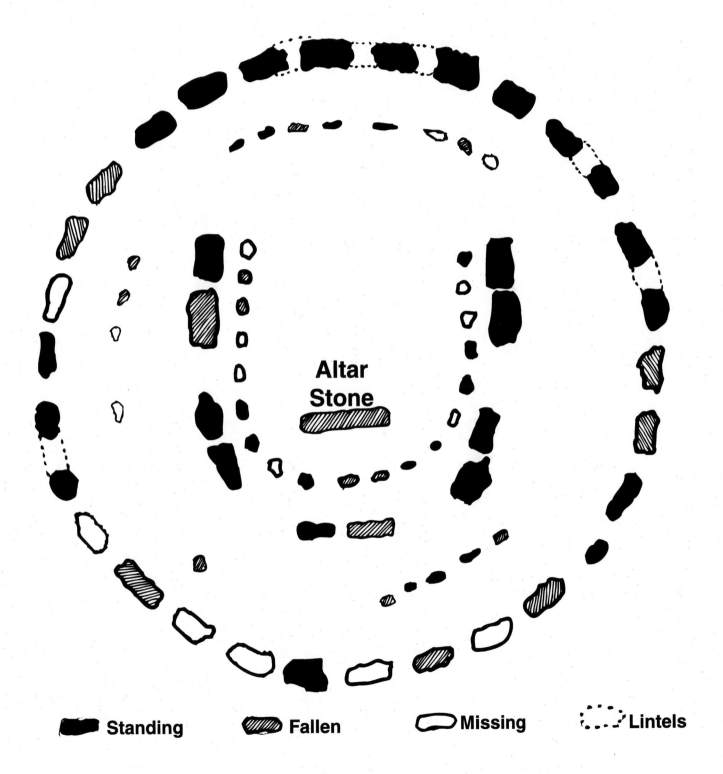

Altar Stone

■ **Standing**   ▨ **Fallen**   ⬭ **Missing**   ⦙⦙⦙ **Lintels**

Recipe for a Perfect News Magazine

Directions: Many people tune into the news each day to find out what is going on in the world. What if television did not exist? How would people get their news? Most likely it would have to be in print. You will be creating a story about one theory of Stonehenge. Your story will be published in a news magazine. Fill in the information below to help you organize your story.

Recipe for a Perfect News Magazine

* ✳ Catchy Title
* ✳ Interesting Pictures
* ✳ Exclusive Interviews
* ✳ Accurate Information

Name of my news magazine: _____

Title of my story: _____

Theory on the reasons for building Stonehenge: _____

What kind of picture will I use? _____

Who will be featured in an exclusive interview? _____

Describe the kind of person that would be interested in reading this story. _____

_____

_____

What information will you use to make your readers draw a certain conclusion? _____

_____

_____

_____

_____

_____

_____

_____

A Conversation at Stonehenge

Directions: Who do you believe built Stonehenge? Why did they built it? Why do you believe this? Is it based on the best evidence? Only the monument itself really knows. Pretend the stones at Stonehenge can talk and tell the story. First, decide on how many speaking parts you will have. Then label the stones and write their conversation in the space below.

Is Atlantis a Legend?

Teacher Lesson Plans

Standard/Objective

✳ Identify and use processes important to reconstructing and reinterpreting the past, such as using a variety of sources; providing, validating, and weighing evidence for claims; checking credibility of sources; and searching for causality. (NCSS)

✳ Acting as jurors, students will hear information that proves and disproves the lost continent of Atlantis and will make a decision on its existence.

Materials

copies of *Attention Grabber* (page 59); copies of *Graphic Organizer* (page 60); copies of *Mapping Atlantis* (page 61); copies of *Background Information* (pages 62–63); copies of *Vote* (page 67); copies of *The Case for Atlantis* (page 64); copies of *The Case Against Atlantis* (page 65); copies of *Juror Speech* (page 66)

Discussion Questions

✳ What are some things these comic-strip stories have in common?

✳ According to the comic-book cover, who is (are) the main character(s)?

✳ What kind of story will this be: nonfiction, science fiction, or historical fiction? How do you know?

✳ What is Atlantis?

✳ What do you know about Atlantis?

✳ What would you like to know about Atlantis?

The Activity: Day 1

Place a copy of *Attention Grabber* (page 59) on every student's desk. It is a front cover page to a popular comic book printed over 30 years ago called *The Man from Atlantis*. Give students a few moments to look at it, and then have them choose a partner for the following activity.

Explain to the class that they will be writing the comic for the story found within this comic book. Their comic strips should be between four and eight frames. It should tell the story of the man from Atlantis. Explain to students that they will have about 20 minutes to complete this comic strip. (You can provide more time depending on the class's needs.) When students have finished their comic strips, let them share their work with the entire class

Teacher Lesson Plans *(cont.)*

The Activity: Day 1 *(cont.)*

Have students look back at *Attention Grabber*. Distribute copies of *Mapping Atlantis* (page 61). Then ask the discussion questions listed above. For the last two questions, students will record their ideas on their graphic organizers (page 60). This graphic organizer is a KWL chart and will help students organize their thoughts, questions, and answers as they study the topic of Atlantis. Remind students to keep this graphic organizer handy throughout the week as they continue to learn about this topic.

The Activity: Day 2

Begin by reminding them about the discussion from the previous lesson. Have students review their graphic organizers. Then distribute copies of *Background Information* (pages 62–63). Let students read it with a partner. Remind students to record any important information on their graphic organizers as they read. Bring the class back together for students to ask questions.

Tell students that they will be treating this course of study much like a trial. Atlantis will be tried in the class courtroom to see whether it actually existed. Distribute copies of *Mapping Atlantis* (page 61) so that students will know the location. Explain that the following day they will first hear the case that Atlantis did exist. The class will be acting as jurors in this case and decide the truth about Atlantis. As a juror, they are not allowed to talk about this case amongst themselves. Distribute copies of the student page *Vote* (page 67). Have students record their opinions on whether Atlantis ever existed. Keep these votes confidential.

The Activity: Day 3

Remind students of the jury instructions. Tell students that they will be reviewing evidence from the case today. Distribute copies of *The Case for Atlantis* (page 64). Simply read the information aloud, but do not allow students to talk about the case or ask any questions. Let students fill in any additional information needed on their graphic organizers from the previous day. At the end of the class period, distribute the voting page (page 67) and collect these papers. This vote should be kept confidential. Remind students of the vote totals from the day before.

Teacher Lesson Plans *(cont.)*

The Activity: Day 4

Remind students of the jury instructions. Tell students that they will be reviewing more evidence from the case today. Distribute copies of *The Case Against Atlantis* (page 65). Simply read the information aloud, but do not allow students to talk about the case or ask any questions. Let students fill in any additional information needed on their graphic organizers from the previous day. At the end of the class period, distribute the voting page (page 67) and collect these papers. This vote should be kept confidential. Remind students of the vote totals from the day before.

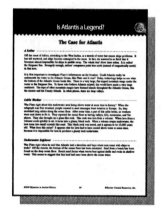
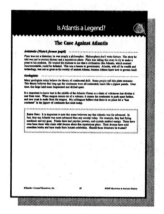

The Activity: Day 5

When students come into class, distribute the student activity sheet *Juror Speech* (page 66). Remind students that after both sides have rested their case, the jurors finally get a chance to talk about the trial and find out how everyone feels. Tell students that they are to present a short (2–3 minutes) persuasive speech in front of their fellow jurors. This speech is meant to persuade the other jurors to their view. Students need to outline what they believe about Atlantis and why they believe it. Give students a few minutes to prepare their speeches. Then let students hash out the case. Everyone should have a chance to present his or her speech. At the end of the class, take the final *Vote* (page 67). This vote will settle the case for the last time. Then show students the vote totals from the previous two days. Ask students to reflect on how their votes have changed as more evidence has been presented. Then ask students to reflect on how their votes changed after talking with their fellow jurors.

Attention Grabber

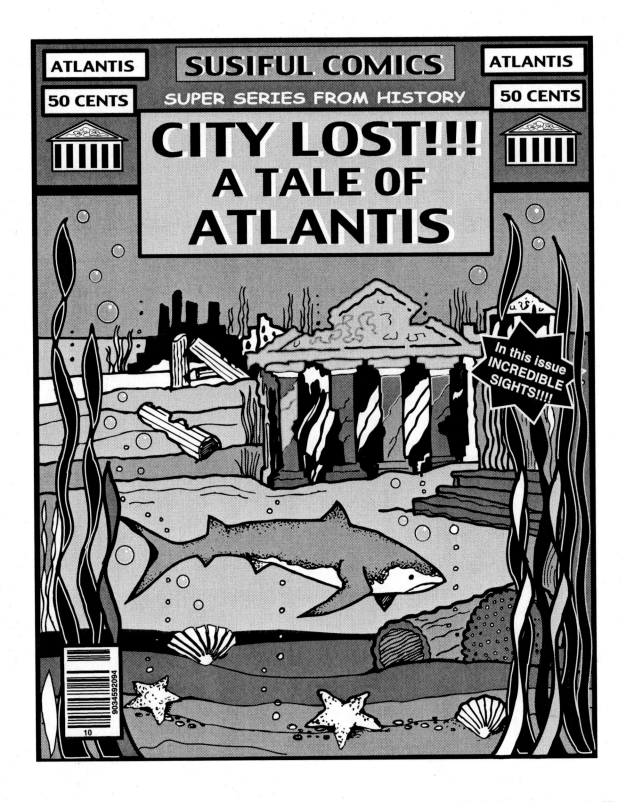

Graphic Organizer

Directions: Use this chart throughout your study of Atlantis. First record what you know about Atlantis under the "Know" column. Then record what you want to know under the "Want to Know" column. Then, when you find answers to your questions, record those answers under the "Learned" column.

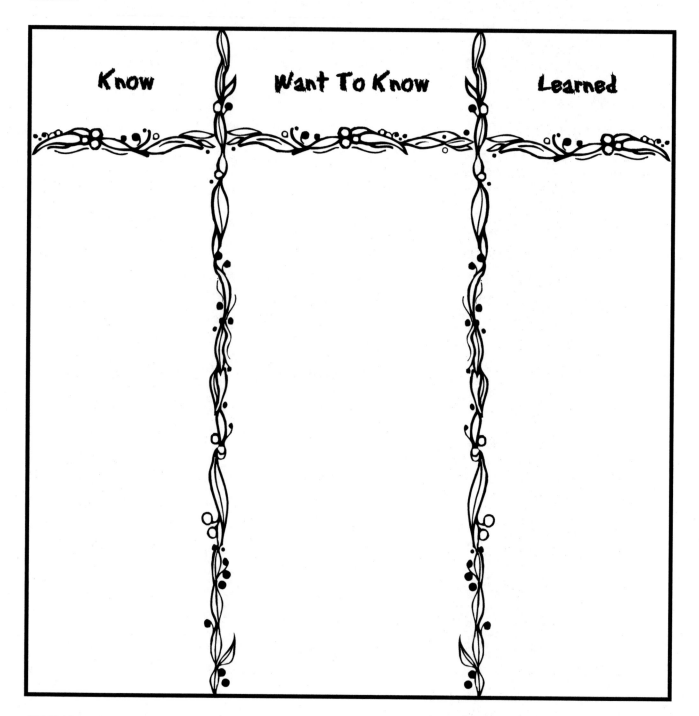

Know   Want To Know   Learned

Is Atlantis a Legend?

Mapping Atlantis

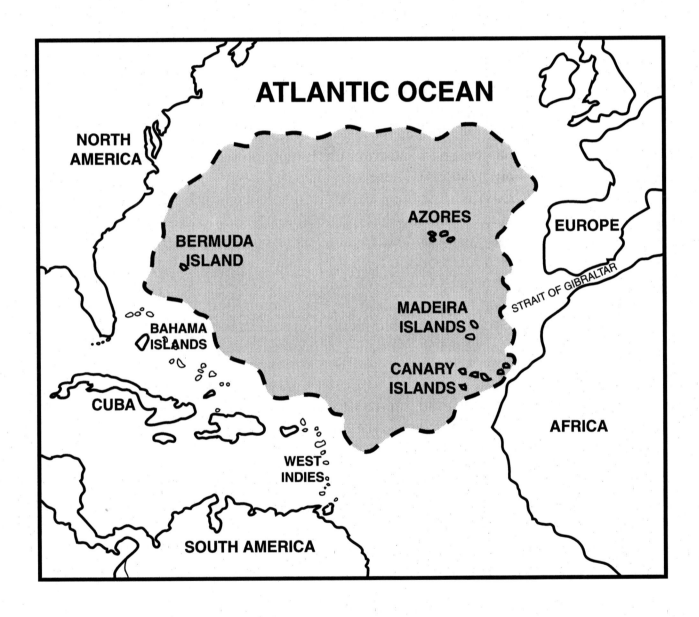

Background Information

How did the Atlantic Ocean get its name? Many believe it came from a lost continent named Atlantis. Did Atlantis really exist long ago? Or are the tales of Atlantis merely legend or some fantastical dream? What evidence is there for this strange lost continent? If it did exist, where was it and what was it like to live there?

The first evidence of Atlantis that modern men know is from 2,000 years ago. Plato, a Greek, wrote about it based on a relative's information. This distant relative was named Solon. Solon was a Greek who traveled to Egypt from Greece to learn about the Greeks. Solon gained his information first-hand from the Egyptian priests who claimed to have knowledge of ancient civilizations. These wise men
told Solon that the Greeks and Egyptians came from an ancient people who lived on another continent, Atlantis. They said that long before a great flood, a huge island existed. This island was bigger than Africa and was located somewhere in the waters off Africa. Solon then passed this story on to Plato's great-grandfather, Critias. Long ago, libraries did not exist for people to learn information from. Stories were not written down, but rather passed on from generation to generation in oral form. To learn, the people listened to stories told by wise old men. It just so happens that Plato wrote this story down. This story takes place as a dialogue between two people. One of them was Critias, who repeatedly states that the story is "literally true."

Atlantis was governed by many kings, one after another. It was envied by all. The army of Atlantis tried to protect their neighboring countries by helping them in wars and conflicts. For that very reason, people loved Atlantis.

Little by little, Atlantis began suffering earthquakes, floods, and volcanoes. Eventually, one day proved to be extremely violent. According to Plato, it was 11,500 years ago. Earthquakes were accompanied by tremendous tidal waves that swallowed people right up. When the violence ended, the continent of Atlantis was nowhere to be seen. It had literally disappeared.

more to follow

Background Information *(cont.)*

Some survived the earthquakes and floods. Those people went to Egypt and also to Greece to start new lives.

Plato described Atlantis as a flat land right in the middle of an island. It had nine different regions with many different kinds of plants, including fruit and nut trees, bright flowers, streams, and animals. Right next to the flat area of land was a large mountain that had hot springs filled with minerals. The people of Atlantis frequently took mineral baths at places all over the island. Gold and copper also covered the land. In fact, there was so much gold that the people covered entire buildings with it!

The capital city was located on the eastern coast and was surrounded by water on three sides. It was a city that survived on trade. The city had tall walls to protect it in case of an attack by sea. Its navy of 20,000 protected its coastline, and its army of 60,000 men protected the land. Most who served in the navy and army were the poor people of Atlantis. It was their job to protect the riches of their land. Others were slaves to the rich. The continent was mixed with beauty of riches and the ugliness of slavery.

The Case for Atlantis

Sailor

Off the coast of Africa, stretching to the West Indies, is a stretch of water that causes ships problems. It has tall seaweed, and ships become entangled in the mess. In fact, the seaweed is so thick that it becomes almost impossible for ships to paddle away. The winds don't blow there either. It is called the Sargasso Sea. Strangely enough, sailors' compasses point true north (instead of magnetically north) in that area.

It is first important to investigate Plato's information on the location. Could Atlantis really be underneath the water in the Atlantic Ocean, like Plato said it was? Today, technology helps us see what the bottom of the Atlantic Ocean looks like. There is a very large, flat-topped mountain range under the water of the Sargasso Sea. To those who believe Atlantis existed, this would have made a very large continent. The tops of other mountain ranges have formed islands throughout the Atlantic Ocean, like the Azores and the Canary Islands. In other places, there are deep valleys.

Cable Worker

Was Plato right about this underwater area being above water at some time in history? When the telegraph was first invented, people wanted to send messages from America to Europe. So, they stretched long cables along the ocean floor. After some time, a part of this cable broke, so workers were sent down to fix it. They reported the ocean floor as having valleys, hills, mountains, and flat places. They also brought up a glass-like rock. This rock was lava from a volcano. When lava from a volcano cools quickly in air, it turns into a glassy, black rock. When a volcano erupts underwater, the lava turns into small crystals like sand. This black rock was tested, and it appears to be 15,000 years old. What does this mean? It appears that the lava had to have cooled above water at some time, because it is impossible for lava to produce a glassy rock underwater.

Underwater Explorer

Was Plato right when he said that Atlantis had a shoreline and bays where men came with ships to trade? Off the Azores, the bottom of the ocean floor has been examined. Sand from a beach has been found on the deep ocean floor. Beach sand forms when waves beat against shells and rocks in shallow water. This seems to suggest that this land had once been above the ocean water.

The Case Against Atlantis

Aristotle (Plato's former pupil)

Plato was not a historian; he was simply a philosopher. Philosophers don't write history. The story he told was not to recount history and a mysterious place: Plato was telling this story to try to make a point to his students. He wanted his students to see that a civilization like Atlantis, which seemed insurmountable, could be defeated. This was a lesson in government. Atlantis, with all its wealth and technology, was not as great as the society of ancient Athens, because Athens knew how to govern itself.

Geologist

Many geologists today believe the theory of continental drift. Some people call this plate tectonics. This theory believes that long ago the continents were all connected, much like a jigsaw puzzle. Over time, this large land mass fragmented and drifted apart.

It is important to know that in the middle of the Atlantic Ocean is a chain of volcanoes that divides it from east to west. When magma comes out of a volcano, it causes the continents to push apart further, and new crust is made from the magma. My colleagues believe that there is no place for a "lost continent" in the jigsaw of continents that exist today.

Extra Note: It is important to note that some believers say that Atlantis was far advanced. In fact, they say Atlantis was more advanced than any society today. For example, they had flying machines and ray-guns. Priests there had psychic powers, and crystals emitted energy. There have even been those who claim wild dreams about this mysterious place. Their dreams have sold countless books and have made them instant celebrities. Should those dreamers be trusted?

Juror Speech

Directions: So, was Plato's story just an invention to prove a point about government, or was it an account of history? Plato's claims through the mouth of his great-grandfather insisted that this story was true. Was it really? Even Aristotle dismissed Plato's story as being merely invented. Only further excavations of the ocean floor and more research from geologists may tell. What is your opinion about Atlantis? Use the all the background information and your graphic organizer to write a short speech (2 or 3 minutes) to your fellow jurors in the space below.

Is Atlantis a Legend?

Vote

Directions: You have heard some information about Atlantis today. Do you believe it existed? Record your vote in the space below. (There will be three preliminary votes and then a final vote on the last day. All of them will be recorded in the space below.)

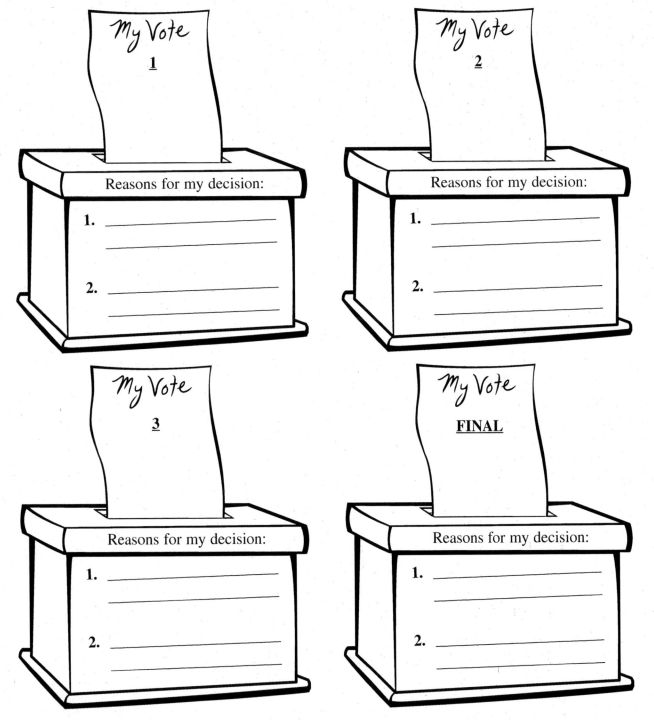

My Vote
__1__

Reasons for my decision:

1. _____

   _____

2. _____

   _____

My Vote
__2__

Reasons for my decision:

1. _____

   _____

2. _____

   _____

My Vote
__3__

Reasons for my decision:

1. _____

   _____

2. _____

   _____

My Vote
FINAL

Reasons for my decision:

1. _____

   _____

2. _____

   _____

The Terracotta Soldiers

Teacher Lesson Plans

Standard/Objective

✳ Develop critical sensitivities such as empathy and skepticism regarding attitudes, values, and behaviors of people in different historical contexts. (NCSS)

✳ Students will create a travel brochure about the terracotta army for the general public that explains the reasons for its existence.

Materials

copies of *Attention Grabber* (page 71); copies of *Background Information* (pages 72–74); copies of *Graphic Organizer* (page 75); copies of *Terracotta Trading Cards* (pages 76–77); copies of *Travel Brochure* (pages 78–79); clay, carving tools (like toothpicks), colored pencils or markers.

Discussion Questions

✳ Describe this picture.

✳ What is the purpose of the figurines in this picture?

✳ Who do you think was in charge of what you see in the picture?

✳ How would it feel to walk around in this picture?

The Activity: Day 1

Place *Attention Grabber* (page 71) facedown on students' desks. Instruct them to not turn it over yet. Begin by having students close their eyes. Tell them to imagine themselves in the scenario that you are about to describe. Read the following to your students:

"You and two of your friends are walking in a field. You are looking for a place to dig a well. You see a place near a grove of persimmon trees and decide to start shoveling the dirt. Your friends pitch in, too. It has been an unusually long dry season. You feel the pressure to find water for irrigating your crops, because if you don't your crops will wither and die. You are shoveling away, and still there is only dry dirt. Suddenly, your shovel hits something very hard. Your arms tingle from the shovel vibrating. Oh, it must just be a rock. Your friends tell you to look a little closer, and you do. You wipe your eyes, thinking that they must be playing tricks on you. What is it that you see? It looks like clay, but not clay that is naturally in the ground. It's baked clay, so someone must have put it there. You brush it off, thinking that it might be an old pot. To your surprise, it is a clay head! You carefully pick it up and look at it. Your friend tells you to break it to pieces because it will bring bad luck if you don't. You choose to ignore him and report the head to the local government. Within a few months, you find out that your discovery on that day is the biggest archaeological find in the 20th century. Turn over your pictures to find out what you discovered."

Teacher Lesson Plans *(cont.)*

The Activity: Day 1 *(cont.)*

At this point, students should look at the attention grabber on their desks. Give students a few moments to look at it and then ask the discussion questions listed above. Then provide students with copies of *Background Information* (pages 72–74). Read it aloud as a class, stopping for questions, if needed. Explain to students that they will be studying the mystery of the Terracotta Army for the next few class periods.

The Activity: Day 2

Distribute copies of *Graphic Organizer* (page 75). Students will be writing down the mysterious aspects of this mystery, their speculations about the mystery, and providing a reason for their answer. Refresh students' memories about the background information from the previous lesson. Ask students to think about the mysteries surrounding this topic. Students can even share their ideas with the class. Then allow some time for them to write information on their graphic organizers. If some students have a hard time with the graphic organizers, allow them to consult a friend for help. Remind them to keep these pages handy throughout the week as they think of ideas about this mystery.

Distribute copies of *Terracotta Trading Cards* (pages 76–77). Have students create a trading card for one of the members of the Terracotta Army. This activity helps students visualize the detail and understand the ranks of these soldiers. Let students share their cards with the others in class. If possible, make copies of the cards and allow the students to have a complete class set.

Teacher Lesson Plans *(cont.)*

The Activity: Day 3

Provide students with a few minutes to record information on their graphic organizers (if needed). Then begin by telling students that they have been commissioned by the Emperor Qin to create a soldier for his terracotta army. Tell them they must first make a clay model of what the soldier will look like. Provide each student with a strip of clay and some carving tools (like toothpicks). Their models must be four inches tall. They can choose to create a general, archer, charioteer, infantryman, cavalryman, or horse (which were Mongolian ponies). They will need to decide whether their soldier will have armor (remember, this signifies rank) or a weapon from ancient times. When students complete their carvings, have the class arrange them in a fashion similar to the Terracotta Army. If possible, take digital pictures of this army to include in the brochure that will be created over the next two days.

The Activity: Day 4

Provide students with a few minutes to record information on their graphic organizers (if needed). Explain that they have been placed in charge of tourism for the Terracotta Army site. Tell them that they will be using the information on their graphic-organizer pages in a brochure on this ancient site. This brochure is certain to answer all the questions about this mysterious site and should include their opinions on these mysteries. Distribute copies of *Travel Brochure* (pages 78–79) to students. These pages will outline the expectations of their brochures. (The actual brochure should be created on a separate sheet of paper.) Provide students with the entire class time to complete these brochures. If digital pictures were taken from the day before, print them out for students to glue onto their brochures.

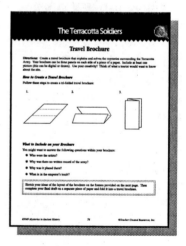

The Activity: Day 5

Allow students to share their brochures with the class. Be sure to point out that the students in the class could come to different conclusions on the mystery of the Terracotta Soldiers. Showcase these brochures in the school library or on a bulletin board for all to admire.

Attention Grabber

The Terracotta Soldiers

Background Information

In the spring of 1974, three Chinese farmers trudged across the farmland of China near Xian (shian). They were looking for a place to dig a well. The season had been unusually dry, and they needed a well to irrigate their farms so that the crops could survive. When these men came to an area near a grove of persimmon trees, they began digging. They dug down 10 feet, but no water was in sight. They decided to continue digging. As one of the farmers shoved his shovel down into the dirt, he hit something very hard. He thought it might just be a rock but decided to investigate anyway. With a closer look he discovered that the hard surface was not a rock, but rather hardened clay. He could tell that this clay had been baked, so it was not just clay that had already been in the ground. It had been placed there. The other two men helped him dig around the hardened clay, only to discover that it was a clay head. It was carved in detail and had a face and hair.

The men suddenly remembered a story several years old. Some of the older village people told a story about a pottery man that was found in the area. These villagers were superstitious and thought this discovery would bring them bad luck. They destroyed it and buried it, in hopes of warding off this bad luck. These farmers did not believe in bad luck, so they took their information to a local government official. In no time at all, archaeologists came out to inspect the area. They not only found this clay man's body, they also found many other clay men, which they called terracotta figurines.

The terracotta figurines turned out to be life-sized soldiers dressed in clay robes and armor. When they were first created, they were painted bright colors of green, blue, red, purple, orange, and yellow. Even the horses were painted! The soldiers' hair was pulled back in a tight knot—evidently the fashion of the day for soldiers. They also had real weapons, like daggers, swords, arrowheads, and axes—which were still extremely sharp. As a sign of their bravery there were no shields or helmets used for protection. More amazingly, each soldier uncovered in the dirt was a distinct work of art. No two were created alike. Each had a unique face. Some were young, and others were old. Their expressions show that some were nervous, others were tired, and some were confident. There were archers, charioteers, generals, infantry, cavalrymen, and horses (Mongolian ponies). They wore the uniforms of the soldiers from that time, which told their rank. The highest-ranking soldiers were the generals. Their uniforms consisted of caps with feathers, tassels, fancy shoes that curled up at the tip, and armor made from small iron fish scales. Those who ranked the lowest did not have any armor. Instead, they wore knee-length heavy tunics, with their shins wrapped in cloth for protection. And what's even more amazing is that there were more than 7,500 soldiers in all, along with life-sized horses and chariots!

more to follow

Background Information *(cont.)*

Who were the artists that created these 7,500 life-sized statues? A few of the soldiers were signed with a stamp, but its meaning is not known. It is assumed that the artists made these for the emperor's eyes only; they were not to be seen by anyone else. Tunnels were dug underground, and the figurines were carried to their appointed place. When all of them were in place, a wooden roof was constructed on top. Then, 10 feet of dirt was dumped on top.

Over the past 30 years, archaeologists have uncovered one very large pit, which is the size of two football fields and contains 6,000 soldiers, all arranged in battle formation facing east. Two other smaller pits were uncovered, with pit two having 1,000 soldiers, 90 chariots, and 500 horses and presumably meant to be a back-up army. Pit three looks like the army headquarters, having what looks like 68 commanders, one chariot, and four horses. They were all facing each other in a U formation, as if consulting one another on the battle plan. Another pit was found, but it was empty. They believe the terracotta army is about 2,200 years old.

Why would there be a clay army of 7,500 men, horses, and chariots buried underground? Who would do such a thing, and why? Archaeologists began to work on this part of the mystery. They discovered that the first emperor of China put them there. His name was Qin Shihuang (chin shir-hwong), and he lived from 259 to 210 B.C. Before his reign, there were separate kingdoms throughout China, each with its own ruler. Many times these kingdoms fought one another, but Qin's army was the fiercest of all and soon defeated the other kingdoms and united them under his control. Anyone who disagreed with him was put to death. To keep dissenting ideas from coming into people's minds, he had all the books burned. He built 4,000 miles of roads to connect his kingdom. He established a common language and currency. To protect his kingdom from foreign invasion, he built the first Great Wall of China, which fortified 1,500 miles of land. Even though he was a fierce ruler, he feared death. He believed that if he could just find the right potion, he could gain immortality. He sent many men out looking for this magical elixir, but they all failed to find it. There were at least three attempts to assassinate him, but he survived all of them.

more to follow

Background Information *(cont.)*

While away from the capital on a tour of his kingdom, the emperor died. He was 49 years old. His attendants kept it a secret, because they were afraid the peasants would revolt if they knew. It took a while to get back to get the emperor's chariot back to the capital. All the while, meals were brought to the chariot and reports were given to the dead emperor so that no one would suspect anything. All of this happened during the hot summer, and a stench began to come from the emperor's body, so his attendants arranged for a raw-fish chariot to ride in front of the emperor's chariot. The terrible fish smell overpowered the smell of his rotting corpse. No one knew that the emperor had died until he arrived back home and they prepared him for burial.

Even though his tomb had been worked on for more than 30 years, it was not complete when he died. Back then, the Chinese people prepared tombs, just as the ancient Egyptians did. They included furniture, clothing, jewels, chariots, and even boats! Qin knew that when he died, there would be those who would want to rob his grave, so he tried very hard to protect his grave. First, he installed some sort of machine that made a large rumbling sound, in hopes of scaring off the robbers. Second, he installed mechanical crossbows at the entrance of the tomb. These crossbows would automatically fire arrows if anyone tried to intrude. Crossbows were the most powerful weapon at the time, but they weren't discovered by Europeans until 1,300 years later.

It was also important for the emperor to have workers who would not tell others where he was buried. He concocted a stone door that sealed the tomb shut after the workers carried his body inside. In that way, the workers died along with him. But this was not enough to satisfy the emperor. Lastly, he had the terracotta army buried less than a mile away from his tomb. It was believed that they would come to life and magically protect his tomb from intruders trying to loot his tomb and evil spirits trying to harm his soul in the afterlife. A large hill was always constructed above a ruler's tomb. If a person was very important, he had a bigger hill. At one time, the hill over Qin's tomb was 400 feet high. That's almost as tall as the biggest pyramid in Egypt. But over the years, weather and erosion have worn this big hill down.

The mystery surrounding this terracotta army is that they are never mentioned in any texts or records from that time. Why did the emperor see the need to keep this a secret? And why exactly is the army guarding the emperor's tomb? What is there besides his body? The government of China has no plans to excavate Qin's tomb, so this may remain a mystery for a long, long while.

Graphic Organizer

Directions: After reading the background information about the Terracotta Army, what do you think are the answers to this mysterious archaeological find? There are several mysteries about this find. First, write down the aspect of the mystery you are referring to. Then, as you think of possible answers, record them on this speculation chart below. You must also provide a reason for your speculation.

Mystery	Speculation	Reason

Terracotta Trading Cards

Directions: The discovery of this amazing terracotta army has mesmerized kids throughout the world. You decide to capitalize on this great archaeological find by creating Terracotta Trading Cards. On the front of the card, draw a picture of this unique soldier.

Front

Terracotta Trading Cards *(cont.)*

Directions: On the back of the card, give your soldier a rank, tell what weapon he holds (if any), describe his clothing, and give any other pertinent information about his performance in battle.

Back

The Terracotta Soldiers

Travel Brochure

Directions: Create a travel brochure that explains and solves the mysteries surrounding the Terracotta Army. Your brochure can be three panels on each side of a piece of a paper. Include at least one picture (this can be digital or drawn). Use your creativity! Think of what a tourist would want to know about the site.

How to Create a Travel Brochure

Follow these steps to create a tri-folded travel brochure:

1.   2.   3.

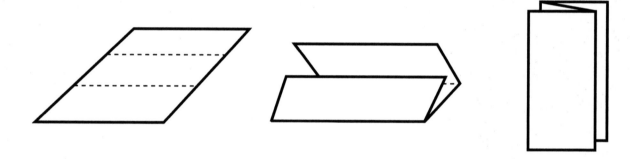

What to Include on your Brochure

You might want to answer the following questions within your brochure:

✱ Who were the artists?

✱ Why was there no written record of the army?

✱ Why was it placed there?

✱ What is in the emperor's tomb?

> Sketch your ideas of the layout of the brochure on the frames provided on the next page. Then complete your final draft on a separate piece of paper and fold it into a travel brochure.

Travel Brochure *(cont.)*

Front Page

1st Inside Page

2nd Inside Page

3rd Inside Page

4th Inside Page

Back Cover

Did King Arthur Exist?

Teacher Lesson Plans

Standard/Objective

* Identify and use key concepts such as chronology, causality, change, conflict, and complexity to explain, analyze, and show connections among patterns of historical change and continuity. (NCSS)
* Students will participate at a Round Table Discussion revealing facts about Arthur's existence and then work with a company to design an advertisement for a historical-figure cereal box that reveals their opinion of the mystery.

Materials

copies of *Attention Grabber* (page 83); copies of *Background Information* (page 84); copies of *Graphic Organizer* (page 85); copies of *Round Table Discussion Information* (pages 86–88); copies of *The Knight's Discussion* (page 89); copies of *King Arthur Cereal* (page 90); empty cereal boxes, paper, markers, index cards

Discussion Questions

* Explain the meaning behind this certificate.
* What are you invited to do?
* How will this affect your life?
* List your qualifications for this invitation.
* What will the discussion be about?
* Did King Arthur really exist, or is he just a character in heroic tales?

The Activity: Day 1

Before students come into class, place copies of *Attention Grabber* (page 83) on the students' desks. Make sure you have filled in a name on each certificate. Give students a few moments to read their certificates when they arrive in class. Then ask the discussion questions above.

Have a large sheet of paper in front of the classroom with the outline of a body on it. Tell students that this body represents King Arthur. Ask students to think about King Arthur. What do they know about him? Invite students to write on the body outline all the ideas and facts that they know about Arthur. If possible, read a portion of a story about King Arthur to your students so that they will have some background on him.

Explain to students that they will have a Round Table Discussion each day of this lesson. As a knight who has specialized in Arthur's Round Table, they will each contribute a piece of information about this mystery into Arthur's existence. If students have the time and means, encourage them to research more about Arthur before the next class meeting.

As a sidenote, have students bring in empty cereal boxes over the next few days for the culminating activity.

Did King Arthur Exist?

Teacher Lesson Plans *(cont.)*

The Activity: Day 2

Begin by distributing *Background Information* (page 84) to students. This page gives students a brief history of the legend of King Arthur. Read this information as a class and allow students to add information to the body outline chart at the front of the room.

Distribute copies of *Graphic Organizer* (page 85). Explain that this is where they will record the information presented at the Round Table Discussions. They will be referring back to this information throughout the investigation. It is important that they keep this page in a safe place throughout the week.

Then remind students that they will each be receiving information to share at the Round Table Discussion. Divide the students into two groups. Distribute a section of *Round Table Discussion Information* (pages 86–88) to each student. If you have a large class, pair students up and have each pair present the information. Each student will also need a copy of *The Knight's Discussion* (page 89). They are to glue their information section onto this page and then write a summary in their own words to share during the discussion.

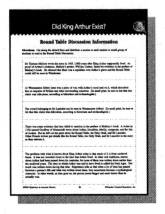 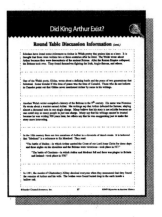 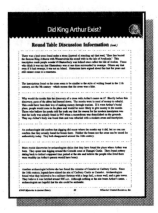

Have students rearrange their desks into a circle. If this is impossible, have students sit in a circle on the floor for the discussions. This way they are sitting at a "Round Table" for discussion. Allow group one to share their information. Remind the class that the rest of the students should be taking notes on their graphic organizers.

The Activity: Day 3

Begin by having students review their graphic organizer notes from the previous day. Again, have students sit at their Round Table. Allow group two to share their information. Remind the class that the rest of the students should be taking notes on their graphic organizers.

Teacher Lesson Plans *(cont.)*

The Activity: Day 4

Again, remind students to review their notes from the graphic organizers. Allow students to ask questions to clarify any information about the mystery of King Arthur's existence. Then tell students that a cereal company has contacted your class for help in advertising. They are marketing a new kind of cereal based on historical figures, and King Arthur is one of them. Since they are all members of the Round Table Discussion, they can offer this cereal company advice and information on King Arthur.

Distribute cereal boxes and copies of *King Arthur Cereal* (page 90) to students. Tell them that this cereal company needs the truth on King Arthur's existence. They are to create a cereal box that tells important information about King Arthur, especially if he lived or not. This is where the students reveal their opinions about King Arthur. Have each student work to design a cereal box for this new King Arthur cereal. (Students can finish this for homework, if desired.)

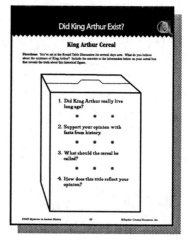

The Activity: Day 5

Students might need to add final touches to their cereal boxes. Allow them a few moments to do this.

Then have students showcase their cereal and explain their opinions about the existence of King Arthur in a final Round Table Discussion. If students forget, encourage them to support their views with the information learned at the Round Table Discussions. If possible, find a place for these to be displayed in the library or in the school office.

Attention Grabber

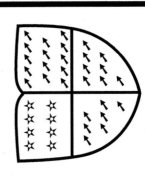

To All and Singular,

Nobles, Ladies, and Gentlemen:

You Are Hereby Invited to Join

King Arthur's Round Table Discussion

And Become a Knight — O.R.B

(Order of the Realm of Briton)

With this privilege, you will . . .

☩ Investigate the reality of Arthur's existence

☩ Discuss the evidence of the burial

☩ Debate the authenticity of the Relics

☩ And analyze the motivation of the Monks of Glastonbury

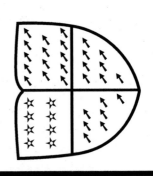

Background Information

Who was King Arthur? Was he a real person? The name "King Arthur" became popular when an English knight named Sir Thomas Malory wrote stories about him. In these stories, Arthur was the famous king from long ago. He was the secret son born to King Uther Pendragon and came to power during a civil war in Britain. He was the one who drew the sword from the stone. He was given another sword called Excalibur when Merlin, a magician, led Arthur to a lake where he received the sword from a mysterious hand reaching up through the water. This sword ensured a victory in each and every battle. Merlin was his tutor, and he helped Arthur to know how to be a good king. Arthur restored peace to Britain and conquered the nations around them. With his popularity, knights from all over flocked to be a part of his round table. They used their might to conquer witches, dragons, giants, and black knights. With the Knights of the Round Table there, the maidens, old people, nobles, and peasants were able to live in peace and go about their business without any fear. Arthur's knights almost found the Holy Grail, the cup that was used by Christ at the Last Supper. His best friend (Sir Lancelot's) love affair with his wife was exposed in court, and Arthur banished him away. He then fell into the evil schemes of Sir Mordred, a knight on his court who was out to ruin him. In a terrible battle, Arthur was mortally wounded. He ordered his sword, Excalibur, to be thrown back into the lake. A hand reached up from the water to take it back, and then a barge sailed into the harbor and took the body of Arthur to the Island of Avalon so that his wounds could heal. It is not known for sure if King Arthur died of his wounds or of something else, but somehow he did die, and his wife was buried next to him at Glastonbury.

For centuries, people have enjoyed this story of heroism and betrayal. No one can fully believe the story as it stands. But is it completely a fairytale, or is there some truth to the existence of King Arthur?

Graphic Organizer

Directions: This is your official notepad. Use this page to take notes at the Round Table Discussion. Organize your notes into two columns, as shown below.

Arthur Really Lived | Arthur Never Lived

Did King Arthur Exist?

Round Table Discussion Information

Directions: Cut along the dotted lines and distribute a section to each student or small group of students to read at the Round Table Discussion.

Sir Thomas Malory wrote his story in 1485, 1,000 years after King Arthur supposedly lived. As proof of Arthur's existence, Malory's printer, William Caxton, listed his evidence in the preface of Malory's book. He claimed that there was a sepulcher over Arthur's grave and his Round Table could still be seen in Winchester.

At Westminster Abbey there was a piece of wax with Arthur's royal seal on it, which described him as emperor of Britain and other surrounding countries. (In small print, be sure to list that this claim was ridiculous, according to historians and archaeologists.)

The sword belonging to Sir Lancelot can be seen in Westminster Abbey! (In small print, be sure to list that this claim was ridiculous, according to historians and archaeologists.)

There was some evidence that they failed to mention in the preface of Mallory's book. In 1136 a writer named Geoffrey of Monmouth wrote about Arthur, Excalibur, Merlin, conquests, and the Isle of Avalon. But he left out the parts about the Round Table, the Holy Grail, and Sir Lancelot. Other French writers put details like the Round Table, the Holy Grail, and Sir Lancelot in the story as they rewrote it.

The problem with what is known about King Arthur today is that much of it is from medieval times. It was not recorded closer to the time that Arthur lived. In other oral traditions, stories about Arthur had been passed down for centuries, but none of them was written down earlier than the medieval years. The time in which Arthur was said to have lived is called the Dark Ages. Not much was written down during that time. Experience tells us that when a lot of time has passed between a person's life and what was written about him or her, that person sometimes become a mythological character. In other words, as time goes on, the person seems bigger and more heroic than he actually was.

Round Table Discussion Information *(cont.)*

Scholars have found some references to Arthur in Welsh poetry that praises him as a hero. It is thought that these were written two or three centuries after he lived. The Welsh wrote about Arthur because they were descendents of the ancient Britons. After the Roman Empire collapsed, the Britons took over. They found themselves fighting the Irish, Anglo-Saxons, and others.

One of the Welsh poets, Gildas, wrote about a defining battle and the peace of two generations that followed. Some wonder if this time of peace was the time of Camelot. Those who do not believe in Camelot point out that Gildas never mentioned Arthur by name in his writings.

Another Welsh writer compiled a history of the Britons in the 9th century. His name was Nennius. He wrote about a warrior named Arthur. His writings say that Arthur defeated the Saxons, slaying almost a thousand men in one single charge. Many believe that his story is not reliable because no one could slay so many people in just one charge. Many say that his writings cannot be trusted because he was writing 300 years later, but others say that he was exaggerating just to make the story more interesting.

In the 10th century there are two mentions of Arthur in a chronicle of dated events. It is believed that "Medraut" is a reference to Sir Mordred. They read:

"The battle of Badon—in which Arthur carried the Cross of our Lord Jesus Christ for three days and three nights on his shoulders and the Britons were victorious—took place in 517."

"The battle of Camlann—in which Arthur and Medraut fell and there was plague in Britain and Ireland—took place in 538."

In 1191, the monks of Glastonbury Abbey shocked everyone when they announced that they found the remains of Arthur and his wife. The bodies were found buried deep in the earth inside a hollow oak.

Round Table Discussion Information *(cont.)*

There was a lead cross found under a stone (instead of standing up) that read, "Here lies buried the famous King Arthurus with Wennevereia his second wife in the isle of Avallonia." This inscription made people wonder if Glastonbury was indeed once called the isle of Avalon. Those who think it was say that Glastonbury was at one time surrounded by swamps. Others say that even if it had swamps, it was not an island. Historians have argued about this fact for years and still cannot come to a consensus.

The inscriptions found on the cross seem to be similar to the style of writing found in the 11th century, not the 5th century—which means that the cross was a fake.

Why would the monks fake the discovery of a cross with Arthur's name on it? Shortly before this discovery, parts of the abbey had burned down. The monks were in need of money to rebuild. This could have been their way of making money through tourism. If it were Arthur's burial place, people would come to the place and would be more likely to give money to the monks. Those who believe the monks told the truth say that the reason for the modern inscription was that the body was actually found in 945 when a mausoleum was demolished on the grounds. They say Arthur's body was found then and was reburied with a modern cross and inscription.

An archaeologist did confirm that digging did occur where the monks say it did, but no one can confirm that they actually found the bones there. Neither the bones nor the cross can be tested for authenticity today. They both disappeared around the 16th century.

More recent discoveries by archaeologists claim that they have found the place where Arthur was born. They spent time digging around the Cornish coast at Tintagel Castle. They found pottery dating back to Arthur's supposed time period at the site and believe the people who lived there were wealthy (as Arthur's parents would have been).

Another archaeologist believes she has found the remains of Camelot at Cadbury Castle. Since the 16th century, legends have related the site of Cadbury Castle as Camelot. Archaeologists found what they believed to be a military fortress with a large hall, a stone wall, and a gate tower. They believe it was fortified around 500 A.D. Although nothing at the site bears Arthur's name, archaeologists are hopeful that the site could be authentic.

The Knight's Discussion

Directions: As a valuable member of King Arthur's Round Table, you have important information as to the reality of King Arthur. Take the information and glue it below. You will present this information to the other knights at the Round Table discussion. Summarize your information in your own words on the lines below.

_____

_____

_____

_____

_____

_____

_____

_____

_____

_____

_____

King Arthur Cereal

Directions: You've sat at the Round Table Discussion for several days now. What do you believe about the existence of King Arthur? Include the answers to the information below on your cereal box that reveals the truth about this historical figure.

1. Did King Arthur really live long ago?

   ✠ ✠ ✠

2. Support your opinion with facts from history.

   ✠ ✠ ✠

3. What should the cereal be called?

   ✠ ✠ ✠

4. How does this title reflect your opinion?

Mysterious Lines

Teacher Lesson Plans

Standard/Objective

✳ Students will demonstrate an understanding that different scholars may describe the same event or situation in different ways but muist provide reasons or evidence for their views. (NCSS)

✳ Students will design a Nazca line for the ancient society and tell the purpose of their design and how it connects to the lines from the ancients.

Materials

copies of the *Attention Grabbers* (pages 94–97); copies of *Mysterious Shapes on a Map* (page 98); copies of *Graphing Lines* (page 99); copies of *Graphic Organizer* (page 100); copies of *Background Information* (pages 101–103); copies of *My Contribution: Nazca Lines* (pages 104–105); masking tape or colored electrical tape, rulers, dark markers

Discussion Questions

✳ Describe what you see on these pages.

✳ What do they represent?

✳ How are they alike, and how are they different?

✳ Did they all serve the same purpose?

✳ What purpose(s) did they serve?

The Activity: Day 1

Post copies of the four pictures on pages 94–97 all over the classroom before students enter. Tell students to walk around and look at them before they take their seats. Then tell students that they have a mystery on their hands: the mystery lies in these four shapes posted around the room. Ask the discussion questions listed above. Do not provide any answers for students.

Arrange beforehand for students to enter various classrooms or offices in the school. First, tell students they will be working with a partner to survey at least five people about the meaning of these shapes. Have students work as a class to brainstorm some questions to ask those they will survey. Then have students share their results with the class. Vote on the best questions to ask. Have student pairs copy down the questions they will ask. Then send students out in pairs to survey others about these four shapes. Provide each pair with all four of the shapes. Students should take a sheet of paper and pencil to record various ideas from others. When someone gives their opinion about the meaning of these shapes, have students write it down.

When students get back from performing their surveys, take time for them to share the ideas they gathered with the rest of the class. As a class, vote on the best four ideas and list them on an overhead sheet for the following day. Tell students that they will learn more about these mysterious shapes throughout the week. It is important to note that students will not read any background information for several days. This will help them to understand what scientists have to grapple with as they study these mysterious lines.

Teacher Lesson Plans *(cont.)*

The Activity: Day 2

Before class, enlarge the pictures on pages 94–97 for an activity. Students will be choosing a shape to replicate on graph paper. Arrange beforehand with the office to allow students to recreate these mysterious shapes throughout the school on the floor.

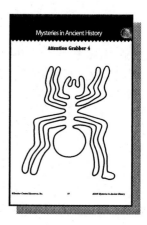

Distribute copies of *Mysterious Shapes on a Map* (page 98) to students. Tell students to imagine they are scientists who have just received a copy of the latest data from the area on this map. It is their job to identify the mysterious shapes on this map. Have students work with a partner to number and identify these shapes on the back of the activity sheet.

Then have the student pairs choose one of the shapes to replicate. Explain that they will be first graphing it on graph paper and then reproducing it on the floor using masking tape or colored electrical tape.

After students have chosen their shapes, provide them with an enlarged copy of these and the activity sheet *Graphing Lines* (page 99). Have students trace over this enlarged copy with a dark marker. Then students should place the activity sheet *Graphing Lines* on top and trace it. Provide students with rulers and tape. Explain that they will be enlarging this shape on the ground. For every inch on their graph paper, students should translate that into a foot (12 inches) on the ground—so their taped shape on the ground will be a further enlargement of the picture.

Explain that they will be recreating these mysterious shapes throughout the school to encourage other students in the school to question this mystery. If possible, have a hallway bulletin board set up asking the school if they can solve the mystery of these lines. .

Teacher Lesson Plans *(cont.)*

The Activity: Day 3

Have students finish their taped shapes today. If possible, allow students to prepare an announcement for the loudspeaker that challenges the other students to solve this mystery

The Activity: Day 4

Distribute copies of *Graphic Organizer* (page 100) for students. Explain that they will be using this page to record information about this mystery as they read the background information. Before reading, they should record information in the K and W columns. Remind students to record information on their graphic organizers in the L column after they read.

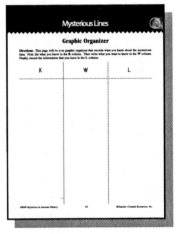

Then distribute copies of *Background Information* (pages 101–103) for students to read with a partner. When students have finished both reading and recording information on their graphic organizers, have some students share what they have on their organizers with the class. At this time, students can continue to add to their information. Discuss the different possibilities. Students might have some original ideas for these lines, too. Have students keep these organizers in a safe place to refer back to the following day.

The Activity: Day 5

Tell students that they will be making a decision about the mystery of the Nazca lines today. Provide students with copies of *My Contribution: Nazca Lines* (pages 104–105). Have students refer back to their graphic organizers and background information for help. When students have completed these pages, allow them to share them with the class. If possible, post their new pictures and opinions on a bulletin board so that other classes can see their ideas. Alert the school to these findings, and maybe others will have ideas they can contribute, too.

Attention Grabber 1

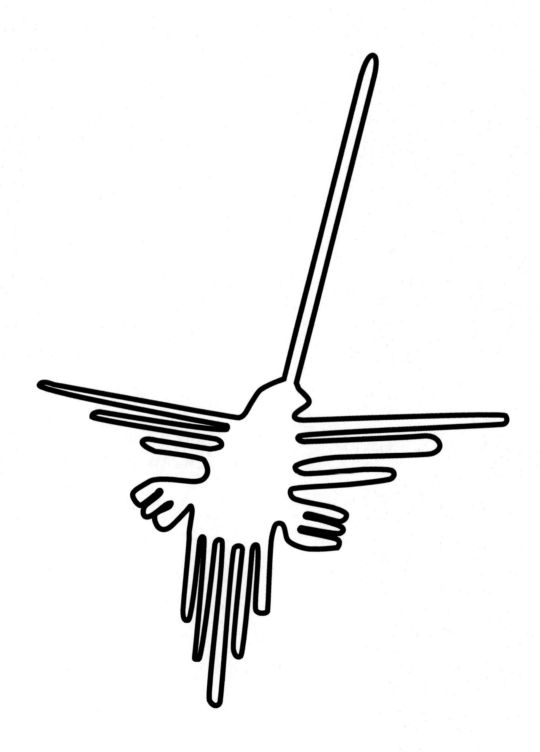

Attention Grabber 2

Attention Grabber 3

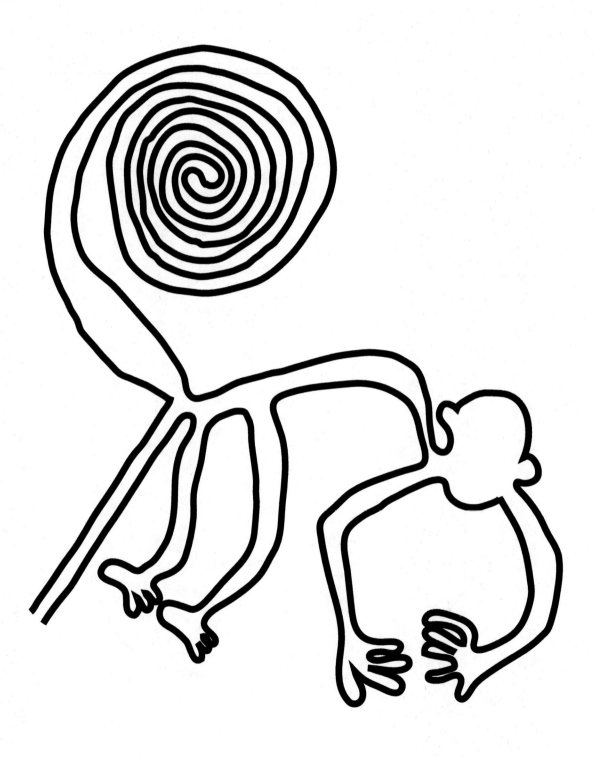

Attention Grabber 4

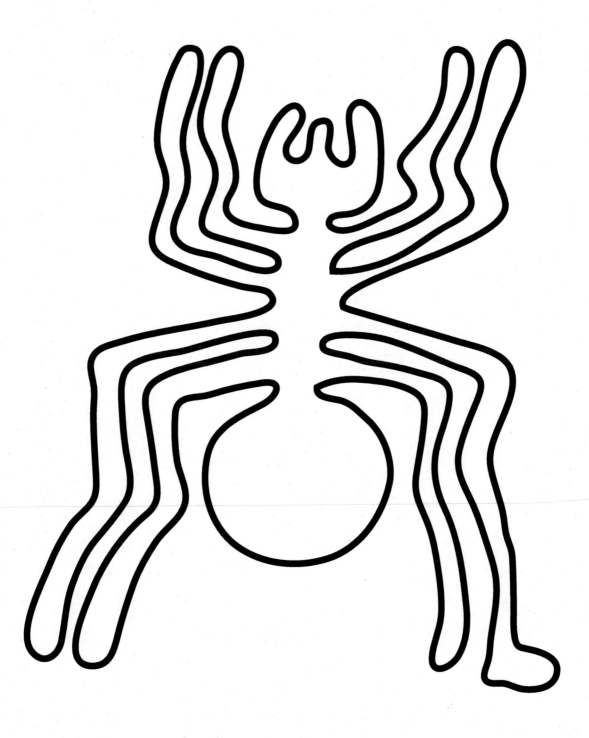

Mysterious Shapes on a Map

Graphing Lines

Directions: Use the graph paper on this page to enlarge your shape.

Graphic Organizer

Directions: This page will be your graphic organizer that records what you know about the mysterious lines. First, list what you know in the **K** column. Then write what you want to know in the **W** column. Finally, record the information that you learn in the **L** column.

K	W	L

Mysterious Lines

Background Information

In the late 1930s, airplanes began making flights across areas of Peru. These pilots noticed something strange: they reported seeing lines drawn on the desert ground in a city called Nazca. An archaeologist from Peru named Toribio Mejia was already working in the area excavating ancient burial grounds. Mejia investigated the area further and thought that these "lines" might be religious roads. He reported his findings at a conference that a historian named Paul Kosok from New York attended. Kosok became interested in these lines, too. He took some time off from teaching and went to Nazca to see these lines for himself.

Kosok thought these lines might be some sort of irrigation canals to water the crops. As he investigated more, he noticed that some of the lines were not straight, but rather they curved around and connected together to form a very large shape. Some of these lines were very narrow, and others were more than 10 feet wide. Kosok had some pictures taken from the air to see if there were any more complex lines. The pictures showed that there were dozens!

In the meantime, a mathematician named Maria Reiche taught in the town of Nazca. Kosok enlisted her help when he arrived in Nazca. He thought her math skills could help him survey and map the area. It wasn't long before she saw some mysterious lines in the landscape, too. As Reiche plotted these lines on paper, both of them noticed that they formed a picture of a very large bird with a tail that was 160 feet long. Kosok and Reiche were both very excited. They knew they were on to something important. Kosok offered Reiche a job mapping these lines, while he went back to New York to teach. She took it and worked for over 40 years mapping these lines. What she found was that the lines spread over 150 square miles. As they published their work, more archaeologists became interested in finding out about the ancient people who made these mysterious lines.

The ground of the desert plain in Nazca and other surrounding parts of Peru is covered in rocks. These rocks have a dark brown color to them. The ancients who made the lines removed the rocks from the ground and revealed the sandy yellow soil. The yellow color helps make the lines stands out. Many of the lines were in shambles because the yellow soil blew away and the rocks blew back into the lines. Reiche worked at clearing the sites to make them the way they were long ago. She noticed that there were also many cleared areas in the shapes of trapezoids or triangles. It was very rare to find a rectangular cleared area.

more to follow

Background Information *(cont.)*

In one area near a valley, 40 lines that made the shape of animal figures were found. This valley was created by a seasonal river that cut through the high plain area. The lines formed the shape of spiders, lizards, birds, monkeys, killer whales, llamas, dogs, and more. She also noticed that there were more shapes in this area than in any other.

Reiche also discovered spiral patterns that were 300 feet in diameter. At the very center of each of these spirals was a small stone. On this stone was a picture of a snake with a severed head. She believed this meant that all the spiral shapes were to represent snakes. She wondered if these lines, spirals, and clearings had something to do with constellations.

No one paid much attention to her or her findings in Nazca. But all that changed in 1963, when many became interested in the mystery of the Nazca lines. Strange ideas and theories about these lines abounded! Some people even said that ancient astronauts created these lines as runways for their amazing spacecraft. Many laughed at these ideas, but the question remained about why the Nascans would make lines that could only be seen from the air.

Some archaeologists believe that the Nascans could have constructed hot-air balloons. In local ancient burial places, lightweight cotton has been found. If it was woven tightly together, it could be made into a balloon. In 1975, an experiment was conducted using this cotton and a reed basket. The two men stayed in the air for several minutes. Although this does not prove that the Nascans made hot-air balloons, it does show that it was possible.

Scientists and archaeologists also worked on dating these lines. How old were they? They have searched for archaeological remains and tried to carbon date them. Pottery pieces have been found in burial sites that date back to between 100 B.C. and 100 A.D. This pottery had brightly-colored animals, including cats, killer whales, and hummingbirds. Other pottery was found 12 miles away and dated from 900–1450 A.D. Based on their findings, many scientists have concluded that the animal-shaped lines were created about 1,000 years before the straight lines—so they were made by two different groups of people at two separate times.

As scientists plotted these lines on computers, they realized that the position of many of the shapes was at the point where the sun appeared on the horizon in early November. November was the month when rainwater from the Andes Mountains began flowing into rivers near the coast.

Background Information *(cont.)*

Kosok and Reiche both witnessed the sun setting at the center of certain lines during the winter and summer solstices. They believed they had uncovered the largest astronomy book of all time. They claimed that many of the shapes represented constellations in the sky. For example, the large spider was the shape of Orion.

Kosok believed that the Nascan society was controlled by a group of astronomer-priests. But archaeologists have never uncovered any architecture, pottery paintings, or burials that show pictures of astronomer-priests.

Reiche believed that the Nascans relied on the stars and the solstices for agricultural reasons. The rivers flooded once a year, and to get ready for the waters, the irrigation ditches had to be cleared and the seeds had to be planted. As astronomers looked at her theory, they plotted the information into their computers to see if these lines matched up with the stars, sun, and moon in ancient times. Only a minority of these shapes seemed to match up.

Other scientists have studied the area thinking that the lines were intended to be walked upon by the ancient Nascans. In other words, they agreed with Mejia's thoughts: the roads were religious roads. Some believe these roads were procession roads and used for special ceremonies. They even think that it was possible that shamans (religious leaders) walked these animal lines hoping to come in touch with the animals.

Some say these lines relate to the rainfall in the area. Since it is a desert area, there was always a threat of drought. The straight lines could have helped lead the water to certain communities in the valley. The cleared areas also served to tap into the water runoff from the hills nearby. They say the animal shapes—which were the oldest of the three types of markings—were the first effort to tap into the water gods of the Nascan society. Some even think that it was an effort of the regular Nascan people without their priests. It is as if they had given up on their priests to pray for the rain and had taken the responsibility upon themselves to contact the gods for help.

No one knows for sure what these lines mean. It will continue to remain a mystery. One thing is for sure: scientists will continue to test their theories and look for more explanations.

My Contribution: Nazca Lines

Directions: You have surveyed, thought about, and mapped your own Nazca lines that existed from ancient times. What do these mean, and why were they created? Create an original shape for the ancient Nazca people. On the following page, explain your answer to the mystery of these lines.

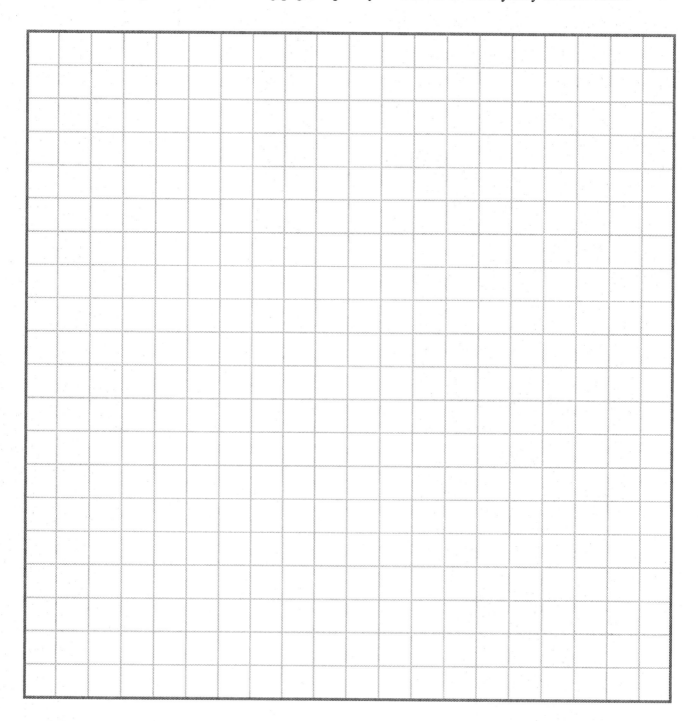

My Contribution: Nazca Lines *(cont.)*

_____

_____

_____

_____

_____

_____

_____

_____

_____

_____

_____

Statues on Easter Island

Teacher Lesson Plans

Standard/Objective

✳ Students will demonstrate an understanding that different scholars may describe the same event or situation in different ways but must provide reasons or evidence for their views. (NCSS)

✳ Students will investigate the statues on Easter Island, create a documentary, and finally make a decision on who created the statues and the purpose for which they served.

Materials

copies of *Attention Grabber* (page 109); copies of *Easter Island Map* (page 110); copies of *Graphic Organizer* (page 111); copies of *Background Information* (page 112); copies of *The Case for Heyerdahl* (page 113); copies of *The Case Against Heyerdahl* (pages 114–115); copies of *A Documentary of Mysterious Statues* (pages 116–117); copies of *My Theory* (page 118)

Discussion Questions

✳ What is mysterious about these statues?

✳ If you were to describe these statues to someone who has never seen them, what would you say about them?

✳ Why do you think someone would create statues like these?

✳ How old do you think these statues are?

✳ How big do you think these statues are?

The Activity: Day 1

Begin this lesson by distributing copies of *Attention Grabber* (page 109) to students. Then write the following question on the board: "Who created these statues?" Have students find a partner and brainstorm possible answers. Many students might never have heard of Easter Island, so don't give away the location of the statues yet. Allow each pair to share their best answer with the class. Have students work with a partner and use yardsticks to measure the height of two of these statues. The tallest statue found was 33 feet tall. The average statue was about 14 feet 6 inches. Allow students to measure the height on the ground, marking end to end with masking tape. This will help students to get a good idea of the size of these statues.

Then ask the remaining discussion questions listed above. Tell students that they will be researching their ideas and coming to a final conclusion on who really created these statues.

It is important for students to first know something about the location of these islands. Distribute copies of *Easter Island Map* (page 110). Have students compare this map to a globe and locate the islands. Then distribute a copy of *Background Information* (page 112). Let students read it with their partner. Take time for students to ask and clarify questions as they read. Tell students that they will be learning more about the Easter Island Statues as the week progresses.

Teacher Lesson Plans *(cont.)*

The Activity: Day 2

Begin with these questions: Who created the statues on Easter Island, and why were they created? Distribute *Graphic Organizer* (page 111). Tell students that over the next few days they will be looking at two different theories regarding who created the statues. They will also need to pay close attention to the reasons why these statues could have been created and then make a decision on what they believe.

Tell students that they will work in small groups to create a documentary for television. This documentary will explore the following questions: Who created the statues on Easter Island? Why were they created? Tell students that they will be presenting this live documentary to the class.

Divide students into two groups. Each group will represent one of two theories: the Polynesians created the statues, or the South Americans created the statues. Half of the class will present one theory, and the other half of the class will create the other theory. Each student will work with a partner to create this documentary. In this way, there will be several documentaries for each side. Tell each group that their goal is to persuade its audience that their theory is the right one. Explain that it does not matter if they believe this fact is actually true. To accomplish this, each group will need to present facts that make their theory look good. They can also use condemning evidence to show that the other theory could not be true.

Distribute *The Case for Heyerdahl* (page 113). This page will explain one theory about the Easter Island statue creators. Have students read this with a partner. Remind students to record information about this theory on their T-chart. Have them keep their graphic organizers handy for the activities throughout the week.

The Activity: Day 3

Begin by distributing *The Case Against Heyerdahl* (pages 114–115). Have students work with their partners to read this selection. Then remind students to record their information on their T-charts.

Distribute copies of *A Documentary of Mysterious Statues* (pages 116–117). Each student will have a job to do: one student will be writing questions to ask, and the other will be preparing to answer those questions based on the evidence found in the reading. Working with their partners, have students choose parts for their documentaries. Each expert prepares information to present on this documentary. Give each student time to work on their activity sheet individually.

With their partners, they also must decide on a format. For example, will the documentary be a formal sit-down, question-and-answer format? Or will it be broadcasting via satellite on location with each expert at the explorer's hometown? Students might want to include a public-opinion poll in the documentary. (If desired, this poll can be conducted as homework. Have students briefly present the evidence to family and friends outside of school.)

Teacher Lesson Plans *(cont.)*

The Activity: Day 4

First, have the entire class create a rubric for judging these documentaries. This can be done on the board or on an overhead projector. Categories can include presentation of each expert and interviewer, information presented, interesting format, convincing arguments, and overall performance of each group. With the remaining time, have students practice their presentations. They should keep in mind that their documentaries will be performed live and judged by their peers on the following day.

The Activity: Day 5

Students will present their documentaries on this day. Give students a few moments to prepare.

It might be interesting to ask other staff and classes to watch the presentations. After each performance, distribute the student-written rubric and let the audience judge the performance.

If available, tape the documentaries using a video camera. Let students watch the presentations again. Ask the following questions:

* ✱ Who had the most convincing documentary?

* ✱ How much power does the media have over their viewers?

* ✱ Do you think that most journalism is accurate? Why or why not?

* ✱ Is it possible to prove *any* viewpoint to viewers, regardless of the viewpoint and its evidence?

Finally, distribute the student activity sheet titled *My Theory* (page 118). Have students complete this page, recording their opinions on this mystery. If time permits, let students share their opinions in small groups.

Attention Grabber

Easter Island Map

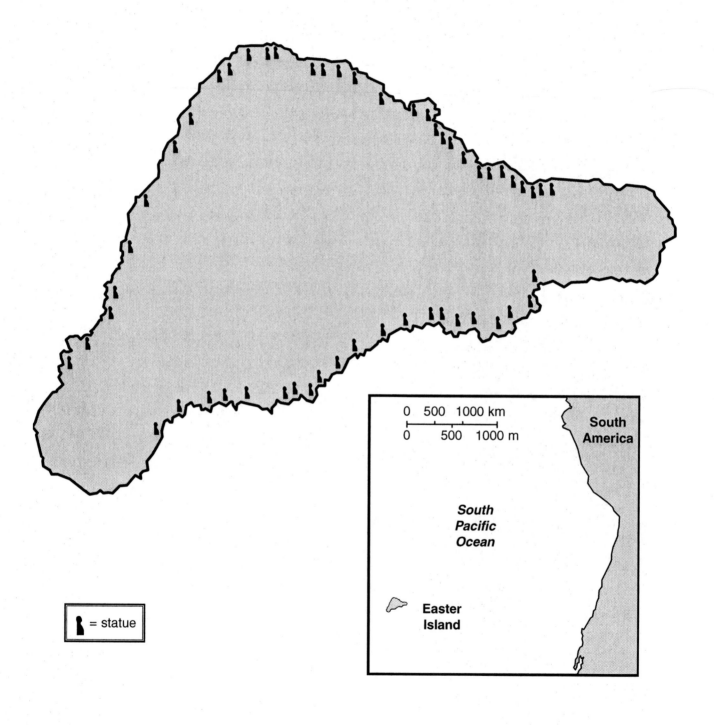

= statue

0   500   1000 km
0   500   1000 m

South
America

South
Pacific
Ocean

Easter
Island

Graphic Organizer

Directions: Use the T-chart below to record and compare the information for both Heyerdahl's theory and the Polynesian theory.

Heyerdahl's Theory	Polynesian Theory

Background Information

Way out in the middle of the Pacific Ocean, an island called Easter Island sits. It is 4,300 miles west of South America and 2,300 miles east of Tahiti. It is what someone might describe as being in the middle of nowhere. What makes this Easter Island so amazing is its huge statues, called *moai*. These statues—some as high as a three-story building—were carved in the shape of men. They were transported to various places all over the island and then erected on platforms.

In 1722, a Dutch explorer named Jacob Roggeveen first saw this island on Easter Sunday. He gave it the name "Easter Island." He wrote about the moai and how he could not believe the people there could possibly erect such large statues. In 1784, another sailor, Captain James Cook, was exploring the Pacific and stopped at Easter Island. He was also amazed at what he saw. He reported the amazing statues, too. Who created these statues, and why were they created? This is part of the mysterious allure of Easter Island that today attracts visitors from all over the world.

The Case for Heyerdahl

Many theories and debates have occurred about the purpose of these statues and who built them. One scientist named Thor Heyerdahl from Norway became interested in this mystery back in the 1940s. After noticing that the Incas had similar legends as did the inhabitants on Easter Island, Dr. Heyerdahl proposed that the inhabitants came from South America. He claimed that these Indians built rafts, sailed there, and then built the moai. The islanders worshipped a white chief named Tiki. Long ago, the Incas had worshipped a white chief named Kon-Tiki, who was driven out of Peru by their ancestors and into the Pacific Ocean. Both Roggeveen and Cook commented on the presence of white-skinned islanders among the brown-skinned Polynesians. Dr. Heyerdahl believed that Kon-Tiki and Tiki were the same chief ruler and that the mysterious white-skinned people on the island were his descendants.

He also pointed out that the islanders spoke of people who pierced their ears and then lengthened them by hanging long weights on the lobes. "The long ears" ruled the island for quite a while until "the short ears" overthrew them. Dr. Heyerdahl pointed out that the moai had long ears. When he asked the islanders where "the long ears" had come from, they said from the east. To the east there is only more ocean and South America. Dr. Heyerdahl also pointed out that the sweet potato was found on both Easter Island and in Peru. Even spearheads found on the island were like those found in Chili in South America. His theory just had to be true!

To prove his theory, he took a journey from South America to Easter Island on a raft that he built. He built the raft from balsawood, just like he supposed the Indians had done. He did not use any nails but tied the nine-log raft together using hemp rope. He, a crew of five others, and a parrot set out from the coast of Peru in 1947. His crew was at sea for 101 days and had quite an adventure fighting off sharks and living on fish. But the winds pushed the raft far beyond Easter Island, and they landed on an uninhabited island near Tahiti. Everyone survived, except the parrot. Dr. Heyerdahl proved that a raft could cross the Pacific, but he still needed more evidence to prove the islanders came from Peru.

Some have wondered at why so many of the statues were toppled. Dr. Heyerdahl pointed to the warfare between "the long ears" and "the short ears." Archaeologists have found many spearheads and daggers that date from before the European sailors visited. Some think the toppling could have had to do with warfare. This, too, remains a mystery.

The Case Against Heyerdahl

When did people first live on Easter Island? According to radio carbon dating, people inhabited the island around the 5th century A.D. This dating also shows that the moai first began going up between 900–1000 A.D. Those who do not believe Heyerdahl's theory say that the inhabitants of the mountain of Peru did not descend from the mountains to the coast until 1000 A.D. Therefore, they could not have been the inhabitants of Easter Island.

Both Peruvian pottery and textiles—things very common in Inca society—were not found on Easter Island. However, Incan pots were found on the Galapagos Islands, a chain of islands closer to South America. The fact that they were not found at Easter Island leads some to believe they never went there.

What about the sweet potato? Botanists say that the sweet potato could have come from somewhere else in Polynesia, which also grows the sweet potato.

Others have analyzed the language on Easter Island and found that many words are similar to that found in Polynesia, but there are a few differences. Some say that the differences are a result of being away for a long time and the language evolving. The written script, called Rongorongo, also has more in common with the script in Polynesia than in South America.

As scientists have studied the skeletons found on Easter Island, they have noticed that the bodies of the islanders were more like the bodies of the Polynesians. Many scientists also say that the stories of the white-skinned islanders were exaggerated by the explorers.

The Case Against Heyerdahl *(cont.)*

Others discredit the stories about Tiki and Kon-Tiki, saying that they were just stories, not factual. They also point out that Dr. Heyerdahl used only selective stories and left out the one about the island's first king coming to them from an island named Marquesas, which is 2,100 miles northwest of Easter Island.

Some believe Dr. Heyerdahl based his theory on the fact that a raft could make it to a far away island in the Pacific, but his raft used sails, while the Incans used paddles when in the water. In addition, the coast of Peru did not have the lightweight wood needed to make a raft or a canoe. Dr. Heyerdahl had his raft pulled 50 miles out from the shore before really setting sail. In this way he avoided the currents that would have caused his raft to be pulled north to the area of Panama. Did his trip mean nothing, after all?

For others, the spearheads are a hard thing to dismiss. The Polynesians were experienced at sea. They inhabited islands like Hawaii and New Zealand. Some think that the spearheads could have come from the Polynesians who sailed to the New World and back home again.

Why were so many of these statues toppled? Scientists say that there may have a crisis of overpopulation. This possibly could have led to the erection of the moai, as a form of ancestor worship. Maybe the islanders were asking for divine help by erecting the statues. When they didn't get it, they toppled over the statues. Nothing can be known for sure, but as different theories are brought forth, they will be tested and tried to see if they are true.

A Documentary of Mysterious Statues

Directions: Fill in the outline below to help you prepare for your documentary. Remember, it is your goal to prove that your theory of the Easter Island statues, regardless of what you personally believe. To do this, you will need to use the evidence wisely. How can you convince the audience that your theory is correct?

> *My group is preparing a documentary to prove that* _____
> *created the statues on Easter Island. I will also answer the question as to why they were created.*

Outline Preparation

✽ List the strong points that should be covered in the documentary about your theory.

_____

_____

_____

_____

_____

_____

_____

_____

_____

_____

_____

_____

A Documentary of Mysterious Statues *(cont.)*

Outline Preparation *(cont.)*

✳ List the condemning points that should be mentioned about the other theory.

_____

_____

_____

_____

_____

_____

_____

_____

_____

_____

_____

_____

_____

_____

_____

_____

_____

_____

_____

My Theory

Directions: What is your opinion regarding the statues on Easter Island? Who created them, and why were they created? On this page, create a visitor's guide to the Island that includes your personal opinion about the two questions above. You can include pictures and any other information to make this enjoyable reading for a visitor.

The Secret of the Iceman's Death

Teacher Lesson Plans

Standard/Objective

* Identify and use processes important to reconstructing and reinterpreting the past, such as using a variety of sources, providing, validating, and weighing evidence for claims, checking credibility of sources, and searching for causality. (NCSS)

* Students will examine the body of the iceman, weigh various theories about his death, and then make a decision on how he died.

Materials

copies of *Attention Grabber* (page 123); transparency copy of *Location of Discovery* (page 124); copies of *Graphic Organizer* (page 125); copies of *Pictures at the Scene* (pages 126–127); copies of *Items Found at the Scene* (page 128); copies of *The Scene* (page 129); copies of the death theories (pages 130–134); copies of *Background Information* (pages 135–138); copies of *Sketching Ötzi* (page 139) transparency copy of *Introducing Ötzi* (page 140); copies of *The Iceman's Death Certificate* (page 141)

Discussion Questions

* Who do you think this person was?

* Why was he in the mountains?

* When did this person die?

* How did he die?

* Does anything at this scene seem suspicious to you?

The Activity: Day 1

Begin by reading *Attention Grabber* (page 122) to students. Ask them to close their eyes and imagine themselves in the scenario as you read it. Place a transparency of the page titled *Location of Discovery* (page 124) on the overhead projector so that students can see the area where the story takes place. Place students into small groups of three or four. Then ask the discussion questions above. Have students brainstorm ideas about these questions on a large sheet of paper.

Distribute copies of *Graphic Organizer* (page 123) to the students. Tell them that this graphic organizer will be their note-taking page on this mystery. They can add to the page items that they think are necessary to solving the crime. Remind students to keep this sheet handy to record information throughout the week.

Teacher Lesson Plans *(cont.)*

The Activity: Day 1 *(cont.)*

Distribute copies of *Pictures at the Scene* (pages 126–127) to show students the items found with the body. Have them work in their small groups to label each of the items. Tell students that if they are not sure about an item, they can always change their answers later. Have students keep these pages handy throughout the week, too.

Draw students' attention to the question of when he lived. Based on these items, did this man live recently? The answer is no. A person who lived recently would probably have a cell phone or a wallet with him. Tell students that the axe was analyzed and scientists found that the metal used was copper. When did people use tools made from copper? Based on this information, have students make guesses about the time he lived. If time permits, allow students to do some research on this question. Otherwise, tell students that copper was popular for tools in the Copper Age, about 5,300 years ago.

Explain to students that they will be looking at five different theories about this man's death during the remainder of the week.

The Activity: Day 2

Begin by distributing copies of *Items Found at the Scene* and *The Scene* (pages 128–129) to the students. Have them take out the pages from the day before titled *Pictures at the Scene* (pages 126–127). Allow students to work in their groups to label the items again using this new source of information. Ask students to share with the class the items that they had labeled correctly the previous day.

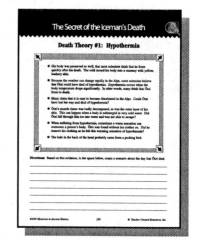

Then tell students that they will be looking at one theory in the death of this man. Distribute copies of *Death Theory #1: Hypothermia* (page 130) to the students. Have students read through these clues in their groups. Explain to students that this is just a theory and that scientists don't know how he died. Tell students to use the ideas from this page to write a scenario of the day that he died. Then allow them to share it with their groups.

Finally, have students take out their graphic organizers and record any important information that they discovered today. Tell students that they will be looking at two more death theories on the following day.

Teacher Lesson Plans *(cont.)*

The Activity: Day 3

Distribute copies of *Death Theory #2: Robbery* (page 131) to the students. Have students read through these clues in their groups. Remind students that this is just a theory and that scientists don't know how he died. Tell students to use the ideas from this page to write a scenario of the day that he died. Then allow them to share it with their groups.

Have students take out their graphic organizers and record any important information that they discovered while reading about this particular scenario.

Explain that they will be looking at another theory in the iceman's death. Distribute copies of *Death Theory #3: Assassination* (page 132) to the students. Have students read through these clues in their groups. Again, remind students that this is just a theory and that scientists don't know how he died. As before, tell students to use the ideas from this page to write a scenario of the day that he died. Then allow them to share it with their groups. If time allows, have each group choose the best scenario and present it aloud to the class.

Finally, have students take out their graphic organizers and record any important information that they discovered while reading about this particular scenario.

Tell students that they will be looking at two more death theories on the following day.

The Activity: Day 4

Distribute copies of *Death Theory #4: Ritual Sacrifice* (page 133) to the students. Have students read through these clues in their groups. Remind students that this is just a theory and that scientists don't know how he died. Tell students to use the ideas from this page to write a scenario of the day that he died. Then allow them to share it with their groups.

Finally, have students take out their graphic organizers and record any important information that they discovered while reading about this particular scenario.

The Activity: Day 4 is continued on page 122.

Teacher Lesson Plans *(cont.)*

The Activity: Day 4 *(cont.)*

Explain that they will be looking at another theory in the iceman's death. Distribute copies of *Death Theory #5: Died in Battle* (page 134) to the students. Have students read through these clues in their groups. Again, remind students that this is just a theory and that scientists don't know how he died. As before, tell students to use the ideas from this page to write a scenario of the day that he died. Then allow them to share it with their groups. If time allows, have each group choose the best scenario of the five and present it aloud to the class.

Finally, have students take out their graphic organizers and record any important information that they discovered while reading about this particular scenario.

The Activity: Day 5

Before distributing the *Background Information* (pages 135–138), have students brainstorm aloud the facts about the iceman. What do they know about him? How did he live? Then distribute copies of this information and read it aloud to the class.

Have students use *Sketching Ötzi* (page 139) to draw a picture of what they think Ötzi looked like, with all his tools and clothing. Then place a transparency copy of *Introducing Ötzi* (page 140) on the overhead for students to see what scientists think about his appearance.

Then tell students that they will be making a decision of how Ötzi died. Distribute copies of *The Iceman's Death Certificate* (page 141) to the students. Have students look back at their notes on their graphic organizer page to help them make a decision about his death. Then they are to fill out the information on this page that tells how he died. Encourage students to be specific with their scenarios about his death. Allow students to post their death certificates on a bulletin board and then present them to the class in a final activity.

Attention Grabber

On a trip to Italy, you and your friends decide to take a few days to hike in the Alps. You have a map to guide you through parts of the Ötzal (UTT-zel) Alps. You are hoping to see the remains of a glacier that has been melting during the past 70 years. You dress warmly, pack your backpack with snacks, and head out for the summit.

After hiking along the trail that many others had traveled that day, you and your friends decide to go another way, just for the sake of exploration. As you walk along, you see something protruding from the ice. At first, you think it is a doll that someone left behind. It doesn't have any hair. You walk closer and see that it is not a doll at all, but a human body. You've just completed your first year of medical school, so you know a dead body when you see one up close. But instead of having waxy skin like most corpses, the body looks yellow and feels leathery, almost like a mummy. It does not have any clothes on, either. It's obvious to your friends that he froze to death. You wonder how long this person has been here. Maybe he was a hiker who lost his way just recently? You take a closer look and see a hole in the back of this person's head. An eerie feeling settles over you as you wonder if the man could have been murdered. You and your friends try to dig him out from the ice with your ski poles.

One of your friends finds a large stick in the ice and begins to dig with it. Then you discover an axe in the ice. Your other degree, in archaeology, tells you that this is no ordinary axe: it is made from some sort of metal. You and your friends believe that the axe might be the key to finding out when this person lived. Suddenly, you see what looks to be a tiny dagger made from flint with a wooden handle. There's also something that looks to be like a fanny pack with a few items still inside! You take out your digital camera and take pictures of these items for later reference. Just in time, too! The authorities have arrived to take all this away to the medical laboratory for tests. You decide to give this person a name. You and your friends agree that he should be named Ötzi, in honor of the mountain where he was found. You wonder, as they take away his body, how did this man die? It is a question that will haunt you for months—and you must find out.

Location of Discovery

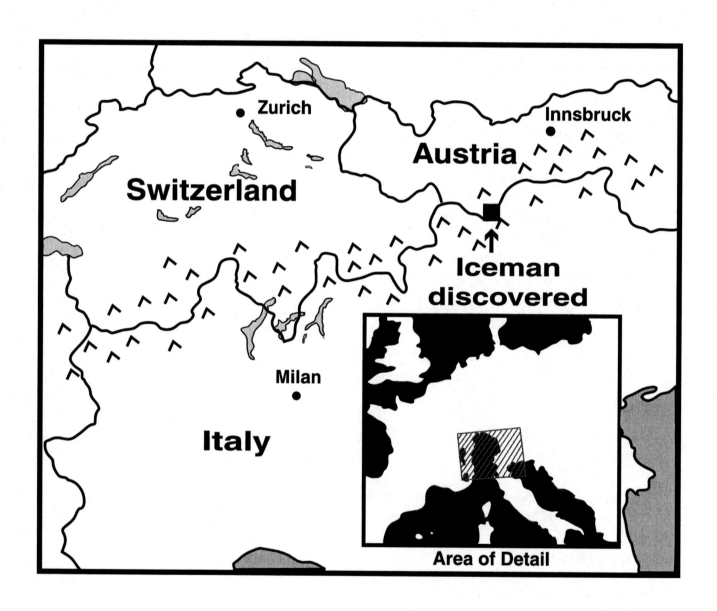

Graphic Organizer

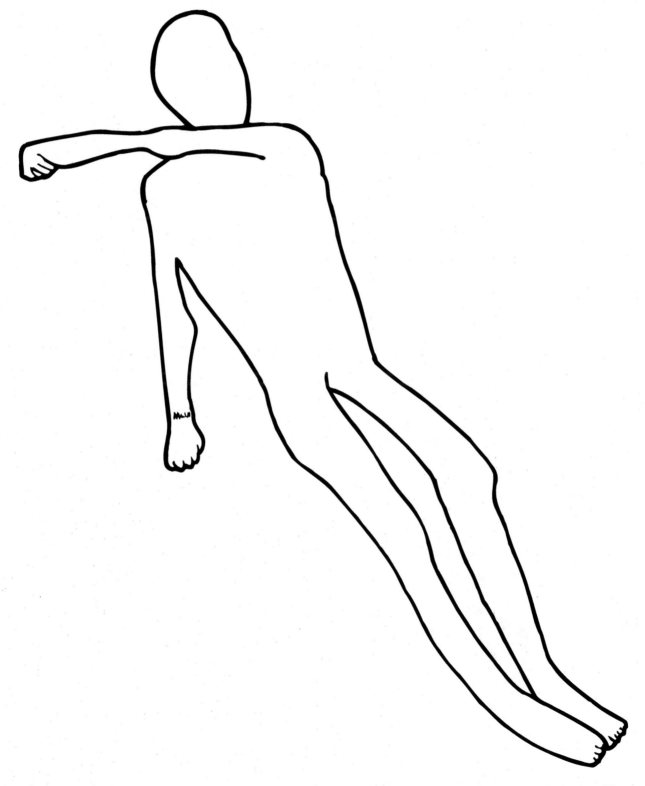

Pictures at the Scene

Directions: The pictures you took at the scene have been printed below. What are these items? Work with your team to try to label the items below.

Pictures at the Scene *(cont.)*

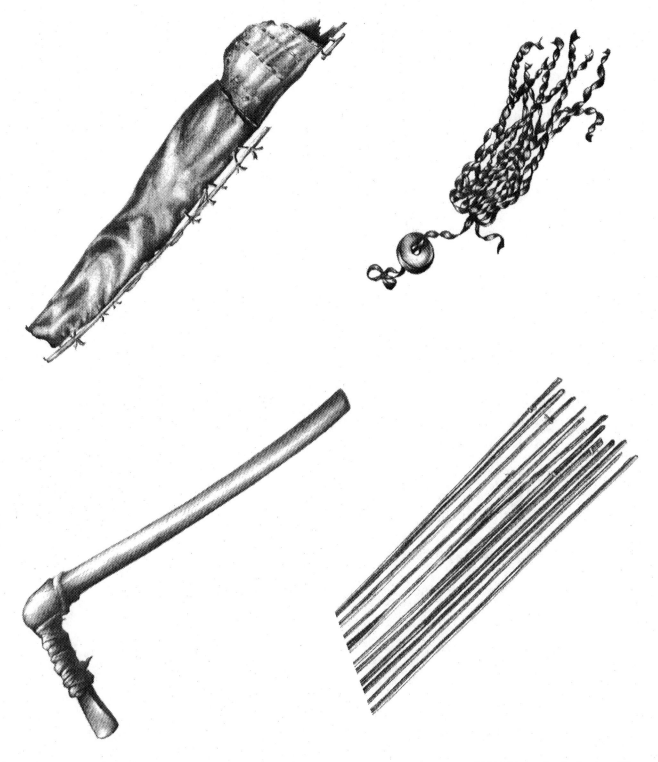

Items Found at the Scene

* bits of leather, fur, and fiber

* 1 cap

* 1 shoe

* 1 bow that is not finished

* 1 quiver with 2 finished arrows and 12 not finished

* 1 axe with a copper blade

* 1 wooden backpack frame

* 2 birch-bark containers

* 1 flint dagger inside of a woven scabbard

* a pouch worn around the waist containing 2 pieces of flint, 1 four-inch-long wooden stick that looked like a fat pencil with a tip made from a deer antler, grass string, and a needle made from bone

* 1 leather tassel with a marble bead

* bits of fiber that resemble a net

* berries and pieces of antelope meat

* mushrooms threaded onto a leather strip

The Scene

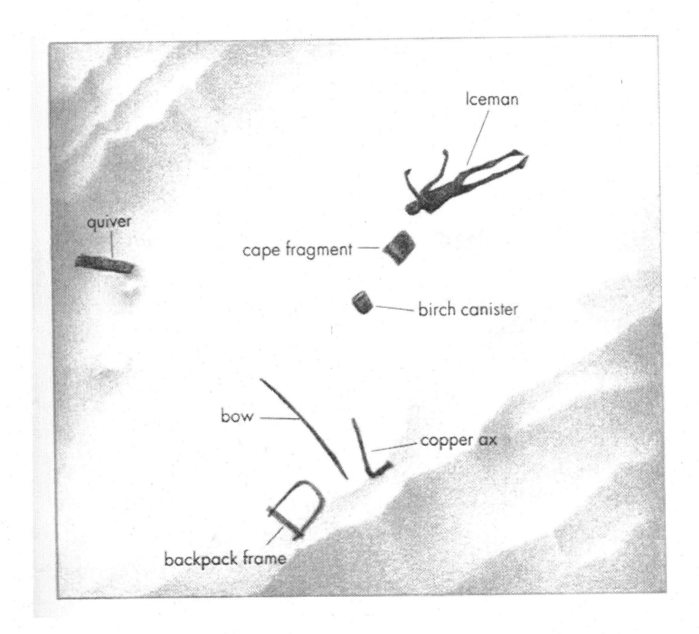

Death Theory #1: Hypothermia

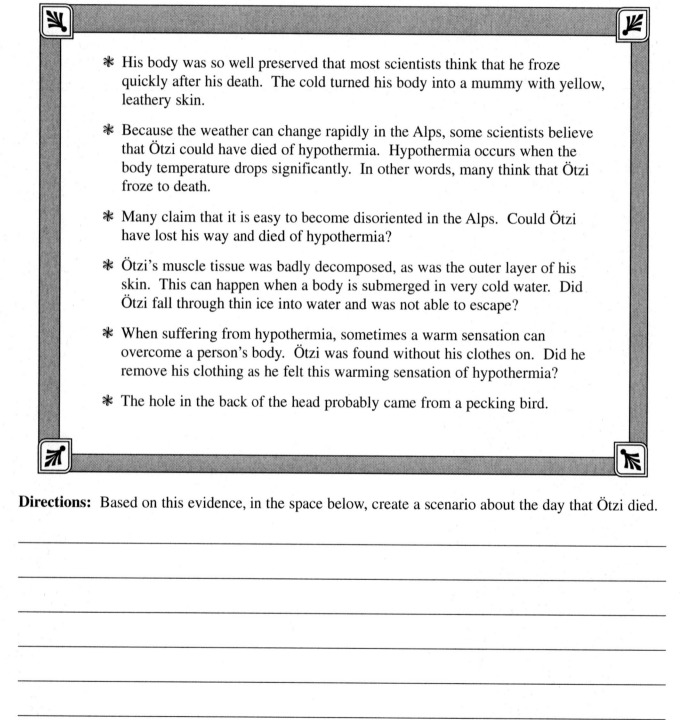

* His body was so well preserved that most scientists think that he froze quickly after his death. The cold turned his body into a mummy with yellow, leathery skin.

* Because the weather can change rapidly in the Alps, some scientists believe that Ötzi could have died of hypothermia. Hypothermia occurs when the body temperature drops significantly. In other words, many think that Ötzi froze to death.

* Many claim that it is easy to become disoriented in the Alps. Could Ötzi have lost his way and died of hypothermia?

* Ötzi's muscle tissue was badly decomposed, as was the outer layer of his skin. This can happen when a body is submerged in very cold water. Did Ötzi fall through thin ice into water and was not able to escape?

* When suffering from hypothermia, sometimes a warm sensation can overcome a person's body. Ötzi was found without his clothes on. Did he remove his clothing as he felt this warming sensation of hypothermia?

* The hole in the back of the head probably came from a pecking bird.

Directions: Based on this evidence, in the space below, create a scenario about the day that Ötzi died.

_____

_____

_____

_____

_____

_____

_____

Death Theory #2: Robbery

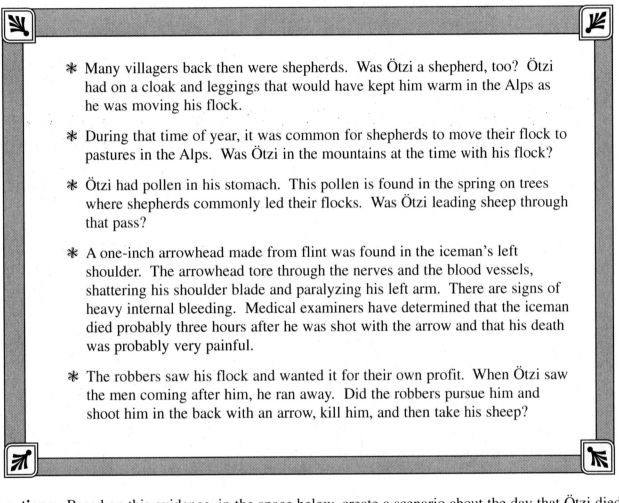

* Many villagers back then were shepherds. Was Ötzi a shepherd, too? Ötzi had on a cloak and leggings that would have kept him warm in the Alps as he was moving his flock.

* During that time of year, it was common for shepherds to move their flock to pastures in the Alps. Was Ötzi in the mountains at the time with his flock?

* Ötzi had pollen in his stomach. This pollen is found in the spring on trees where shepherds commonly led their flocks. Was Ötzi leading sheep through that pass?

* A one-inch arrowhead made from flint was found in the iceman's left shoulder. The arrowhead tore through the nerves and the blood vessels, shattering his shoulder blade and paralyzing his left arm. There are signs of heavy internal bleeding. Medical examiners have determined that the iceman died probably three hours after he was shot with the arrow and that his death was probably very painful.

* The robbers saw his flock and wanted it for their own profit. When Ötzi saw the men coming after him, he ran away. Did the robbers pursue him and shoot him in the back with an arrow, kill him, and then take his sheep?

Directions: Based on this evidence, in the space below, create a scenario about the day that Ötzi died.

_____

_____

_____

_____

_____

_____

_____

The Secret of the Iceman's Death

Death Theory #3: Assassination

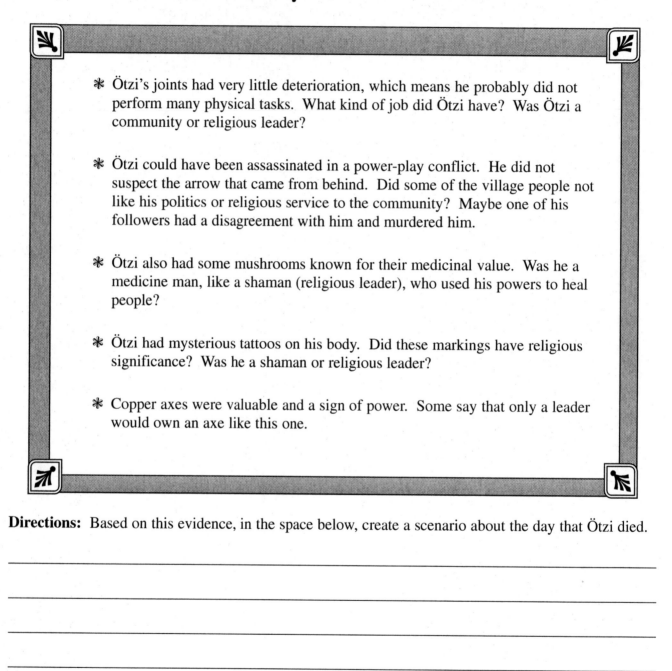

✳ Ötzi's joints had very little deterioration, which means he probably did not perform many physical tasks. What kind of job did Ötzi have? Was Ötzi a community or religious leader?

✳ Ötzi could have been assassinated in a power-play conflict. He did not suspect the arrow that came from behind. Did some of the village people not like his politics or religious service to the community? Maybe one of his followers had a disagreement with him and murdered him.

✳ Ötzi also had some mushrooms known for their medicinal value. Was he a medicine man, like a shaman (religious leader), who used his powers to heal people?

✳ Ötzi had mysterious tattoos on his body. Did these markings have religious significance? Was he a shaman or religious leader?

✳ Copper axes were valuable and a sign of power. Some say that only a leader would own an axe like this one.

Directions: Based on this evidence, in the space below, create a scenario about the day that Ötzi died.

_____

_____

_____

_____

_____

_____

_____

The Secret of the Iceman's Death

Death Theory #4: Ritual Sacrifice

* Ötzi's arrows in his quiver were broken. Societies back then were known for breaking items in ritual ceremonies. Were his arrows broken in a ritual killing?

* Ötzi had a very valuable item left with him: his axe. Why was it not stolen? Could it have been placed with his body during a ritual killing? Was it a gift to serve him in the afterlife? Ötzi's possessions were carefully arranged on a nearby ledge. Were these arranged as a part of a ritual killing?

* The tattoos could have been placed on his body to prepare it for sacrifice. Was he the sacrifice of the community to appease the gods?

* Ötzi's body was found at a summit, a place with beautiful landscape. Landscape has always had a part in ritual sacrifices. Was it a coincidence that Ötzi was at that particular point on the mountain?

* Ötzi had on twine-and-grass shoes, which were not practical for hiking in the mountains. He was carried there.

Directions: Based on this evidence, in the space below, create a scenario about the day that Ötzi died.

_____

_____

_____

_____

_____

_____

_____

Death Theory #5: Died in Battle

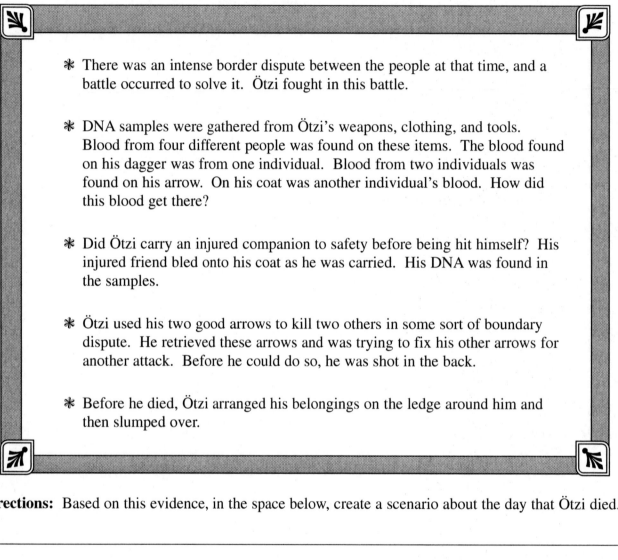

* There was an intense border dispute between the people at that time, and a battle occurred to solve it. Ötzi fought in this battle.

* DNA samples were gathered from Ötzi's weapons, clothing, and tools. Blood from four different people was found on these items. The blood found on his dagger was from one individual. Blood from two individuals was found on his arrow. On his coat was another individual's blood. How did this blood get there?

* Did Ötzi carry an injured companion to safety before being hit himself? His injured friend bled onto his coat as he was carried. His DNA was found in the samples.

* Ötzi used his two good arrows to kill two others in some sort of boundary dispute. He retrieved these arrows and was trying to fix his other arrows for another attack. Before he could do so, he was shot in the back.

* Before he died, Ötzi arranged his belongings on the ledge around him and then slumped over.

Directions: Based on this evidence, in the space below, create a scenario about the day that Ötzi died.

_____

_____

_____

_____

_____

_____

_____

Background Information

On Thursday, September 19, 1991, two hikers in the Alps made a remarkable discovery. Erika and Helmut Simon had been hiking on the border between Italy and Austria. When they roamed off the traditional path, they discovered a small head and shoulders emerging from the ice. At first, they thought it was a doll. But when they noticed a small hole in the back of the neck, they knew it was a human. They wondered if this man had just made his way off the path and froze to death in a storm or if someone had suddenly murdered him from behind.

When they hiked down the mountain, they reported what they had seen to Italian police. The police inspected the site and assumed that it was a recent hiker killed in an accident. The following day, the Austrian police arrived with helicopters and tried to use a jackhammer to dig out the body, which was deeply entrenched in the ice. In the process, they tore the clothes on this person. When their jackhammer ran out of power, they left the scene. In the meantime, the word spread about this body. Hikers and officials made their way to the site and tried to free the body using ski poles and pick axes. One digger found a stick in the ice and used it to try and free the body. He did not know that it belonged to the body stuck there. Other tools were found, including an axe with a metal blade, a stone knife with a wooden handle, a huge bow, and clothes.

A scientist named Dr. Henn was flown to the scene to inspect the body. As he studied the body, he noted that the skin was not waxy, as would be the case with someone who had recently died. Instead, the body appeared to be much like a mummy with dry, yellow skin. It did not take long for him to understand that this was an ancient corpse. Over the past 70 years, the weather had turned considerably warmer, which in turn has caused the glaciers in the Alps to melt. Earlier that spring, clouds of dust from a storm in the Sahara Desert settled on the snow covered mountains. This dust absorbed the heat from the sun and melted the snow around the area where the body was found.

more to follow

Background Information *(cont.)*

Although he knew it would be best if an archaeologist could inspect the area, he decided to remove
the body immediately instead of leaving it there to be damaged by other onlookers. The body was taken to a nearby village and then placed in a coffin. The body was placed in a morgue where it began to grow mold and fungus. The people named the body Ötzi (UTT-zee) because he died near a valley named Ötztal.

Finally, an archaeologist named Dr. Konrad Spindler arrived to examine Ötzi. He sprayed the body with a chemical that killed the mold and placed the body in a freezer. Dr. Spindler inspected the body, but he also looked at the tools found with the body. He was particularly interested in Ötzi's axe. It had a metal blade that he thought to be bronze. Based on Ötzi's axe, he believed that the body was about 4,000 years old, since bronze first came into use then. Dr. Spindler knew that Ötzi was a magnificent discovery. It was the oldest mummy ever found!

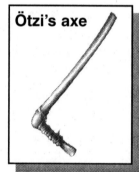

Ötzi's axe

The axe blade was tested, and something even more amazing was found out. Instead of being bronze, it proved to be pure copper. Copper was a metal used by blacksmiths 2,000 years before bronze. Ötzi belonged to the Copper Age and was somewhere between 5,000 and 5,500 years old.

The first metal that prehistoric man used was copper. They found it in rocks, and it was in the rocks at the base where Ötzi was found. Back then, they built underground fires to extract the copper from the rocks. They placed the rocks in these fires and used hollowed-out sticks to blow into the fires. The copper melted and separated from the rock when the temperature reached 2,000 degrees Fahrenheit. The melted copper was then poured into molds. When it hardened, it was used to make tools.

more to follow

The Secret of the Iceman's Death

Background Information *(cont.)*

Archaeologists had already discovered Copper Age villages across the middle part of Europe. They knew that the people there lived in wood-and-mud houses that were built on stilts along the muddy shores of the lakes. These people had carts with wheels and farmed barley, peas, and flax using plows. Besides farming, they hunted and fished for their other food. Animals like pigs, sheep, goats, cattle, and dogs were raised on their farms. They used the barley to make bread and made butter from the milk their cows produced. They were also traders who bartered limestone jewelry for spices like parsley and peppermint.

Although archaeologists knew how these people lived, they did not know what they looked like until Ötzi was found. His bones told them that he was a short man, about five feet two inches tall. He had a bow that was six feet tall. To string and use a bow this large made it clear that although he was short, he was very strong. When Ötzi was found, his hair had not been preserved, but hairs were found in his clothes. These hairs were curly and brown and had been evenly snipped. Based on this evidence, scientists knew he had curly brown hair and that he had just received a haircut before he died. Ötzi also had some mysterious tattoos on his body. One was on his ankle, another was on his kneecap, and another was on his lower back near his spine. Because these were in places that would have been hidden by his clothing, scientists knew they were not for decoration. Some have thought they were religious symbols or some sort of superstitious belief used to ward off pain.

His teeth showed wear, which showed that he ate grains probably made into bread. Inside his stomach scientists found pollen. Scientists believe pollen had settled on his food and water before he ate it. This particular pollen is found on trees in the Alps near where Ötzi was found. Scientists were also able to reconstruct what Ötzi ate as his last meal, just eight hours before his death: traces of wheat bread, a green herb or vegetable, and meat, were found in his colon. He was about 45 years old, which was very old for people of that time.

more to follow

©*Teacher Created Resources, Inc.* 137 *#3049 Mysteries in Ancient History*

Background Information *(cont.)*

The clothes on Ötzi's body also tell a lot about the people back then. Much of his clothing was destroyed when he was dug out from the ice, but enough was left for scientists to examine and draw conclusions. Scientists believe that he wore leather pants along with a jacket made from animal hides. His clothing was stitched together using grass thread. Tied around his neck was a braided grass cape, which looked much like a Hawaiian grass skirt. He might have also worn a fur cap. On his feet were soft leather shoes stuffed with hay to keep his feet warm. A strange leather string with fringes connected to a small white stone disk was found near his body, which leads scientists to believe he could have worn a necklace.

Ötzi also bore a heavy backpack with a wood frame. It was so deteriorated that scientists cannot tell what he carried inside the pack. But they did find a soft leather pouch around his waist with its contents still inside. He carried around two pieces of flint, a four-inch stick that looked like a fat pencil with a pointed edge, a grass string, and a needle-pointed awl.

Near his body lay frozen berries, antelope meat, and two mushrooms strung on a piece of leather. These may have been his snacks. But the mushrooms were known as a type of medicine that fought sickness, so he could have been ill. He had a flint-blade knife inside a grass sheath, which could have been used for cutting up small animals or leather. There were also two strips of felt, which could have been used to start fires. A birch-bark container was used to carry the pieces of felt. Ötzi had a brand new bow that had not even been strung and a dozen arrows, but only two of the arrows were complete with flint tips and feathers.

The question that everyone is asking is, "How did he die?" Theories about Ötzi's death have abounded since he was discovered. At first, scientists believed he was in the mountains with his flock of sheep and he just froze to death. Some thought that he was a hunter caught in a storm and then froze. Some even wondered if he had hurt his arm and could not get to safety. But in 2002, a flint-tipped arrow was discovered in his shoulder just one inch from his lungs. The arrow had entered his body through his back. Based on this new information, some scientists believe he could have died of the wound. If he did die of this wound, who shot him, and why did they shoot him? Even with all the modern technology today, this may never be known for sure. One thing is for sure: there will be more scenarios and theories as scientists continue to study his body.

Sketching Ötzi

Directions: In the frame below, sketch a picture of what you think Ötzi might have looked like. Include several of his tools in your drawing.

Introducing Ötzi

The Iceman's Death Certificate

Directions: You have reviewed the physical evidence in the iceman's death. It is now time to explain how he died. Fill in his death certificate below. Be sure to be thorough and state the reasons for your decision.

Certificate of Death

Name

When He Lived

Occupation

Cause of Death

Further Explanations

Timeline of Ancient Events

20,000 B.C.	cave art
9500 B.C.	earthquakes and floods destroy Atlantis (according to Plato)
7000 B.C.	beginning of farming
6500 B.C.	metal begins to be used
4500 B.C.	Copper Age, copper used in tools
4000 B.C.	plows driven by oxen invented
3500 B.C.	wheel invented
3300 B.C.	Iceman dies in Alps
3300 B.C.	writing begins in Mesopotamia
2950 B.C.	Stonehenge begins being built
2780 B.C.	first pyramid built in Egypt
2000 B.C.	Bronze Age begins in Europe
1323 B.C.	death of King Tut
1300 B.C.	first alphabet
1200 B.C.	Homer's Troy
1000 B.C.	Stonehenge completed
427 B.C.	Plato was born
259 B.C.	Qin Shihuang was born
210 B.C.	death of Qin Shihuang
190 B.C.	beginnings of Nazca lines
400 B.C.	Easter Island is inhabited
500 A.D.	King Arthur
900 A.D.	Moai are erected on Easter Island
1136 A.D.	Geoffrey of Monmouth wrote about Arthur, Excalibur, and Merlin
1485 A.D.	Sir Thomas Malory wrote *Le Morte D'Arthur*

Bibliography

Books

Aron, Paul. *Unsolved Mysteries of History.* Wiley, 2000.

Brier, Bob. *The Murder of Tutankhamen.* Berkley Trade, 1999.

Bryce, Trevor. *The Kingdom of the Hittites.* Oxford UP, 1999.

Cooper, Margaret. *Exploring the Ice Age.* Atheneum, 2001.

El Mahdy, Christine. *Tutankhamen: the Life and Death of the Boy King.* St. Martins Press, 2000.

Fagan, Brian. *The Seventy Great Mysteries of the Ancient World.* Thames and Hudson, 2001.

Getz, David. *Frozen Man.* Henry Holt, 1996.

Humphries, Tudor. *DK Classics: King Arthur.* Darling Kindersley Publishing, 1998.

James, Peter and Thorpe, Nick. *Ancient Mysteries.* Ballantine Books, 2001.

Lessem, Don. *The Iceman.* Knopf Books for Young Readers, 1994.

Mass, Wendy. *Stonehenge.* Lucent Books, 1998.

McMullen, David. *Atlantis: The Missing Continent.* Steck-Vaughn, 1977.

————. *Mystery in Peru: The Lines of Nazca.* Raintree Pub., 1977.

O'Connor Jane. *The Emperor's Silent Army.* Viking Books, 2002.

Patent, Dorothy Hinshaw. *Secrets of the Ice Man.* Benchmark Books, 1998.

Smith, A.G. *The Story of Stonehenge and Other Megalithic Sites.* Dover Publications, 2004.

Sutcliff, Rosemary. *Black Ships Before Troy: the Story of the Iliad.* Frances Lincoln Childrens Books, 2000.

————. *The Wanderings of Odysseus: the Story of the Odyssey.* Frances Lincoln Childrens Books, 2005.

Ventura, Piero. *In Search of Troy.* Silver Burdett Press, 1985.

Wood, Michael. *In Search of the Trojan War.* University of California Press, 1998.

Bibliography *(cont.)*

Websites

✳ **Egyptian information**

http://www.neferchichi.com/

✳ **Iceman**

http://dsc.discovery.com/convergence/iceman/interactive/interactive.html

✳ **King Arthur**

http://www.dryden.k12.ny.us/MediaCenter/MSHS/projects/etrumbull1.html

✳ **Nazca**

http://www.mnsu.edu/emuseum/prehistory/latinamerica/south/cultures/nazca.html

✳ **Stonehenge, England**

http://www.arthistory.sbc.edu/sacredplaces/stonehenge.html

✳ **Terracotta Soldiers**

http://www.travelchinaguide.com/picture/shaanxi/xian/terra_cotta_warriors/pit3/

http://www.historylink101.net/china/terracotta-warriors.htm

✳ **Trojan War**

http://www.stanford.edu/~plomio/history.html

✳ **King Tutankhamen**

http://homepage.powerup.com.au/~ancient/tut2.htm

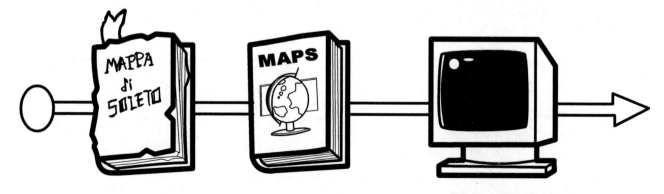